KEYS TO PURCHASING A CONDO OR A CO-OP

Second Edition

BARRON'S
BUSINESS KEYS

KEYS TO PURCHASING A CONDO OR A CO-OP

Second Edition

Jack P. Friedman, Ph.D., C.P.A., M.A.I.
Real Estate Consultant
Dallas, Texas

Jack C. Harris, Ph.D.
Professor and Economist
Real Estate Center
Texas A&M University
College Station, Texas

BARRON'S

All inquiries should be addressed to:
Barron's Educational Series, Inc.
250 Wireless Boulevard
Hauppauge, NY 11788
http://www.barronseduc.com

Library of Congress Catalog Card Number 00-041371

International Standard Book Number 0-7641-1305-4

Library of Congress Cataloging-in-Publication Data
Friedman, Jack P.
    Keys to purchasing a condo or a co-op / Jack P. Friedman, Jack C.
    Harris.—2nd ed.
        p. cm.—(Barron's business keys)
    Includes index.
    ISBN 0-7641-1305-4
    1. Condominiums. 2. Apartment houses, Cooperative. 3. Dwellings—
Purchasing. 4. Real estate business. I. Harris, Jack C., 1945–   II. Title.
III. Series.
  HD1390.5.F75 2000
  643'.12—dc21

                                                          00-041371
                                                          CIP

PRINTED IN THE UNITED STATES OF AMERICA

9 8 7 6 5 4 3 2 1

TABLE OF CONTENTS

DEDICATION

To my late Aunt Miriam,
friend and mentor,
with appreciation for
her support and encouragement.

JPF

1

THERE IS A CONDO FOR (ALMOST) EVERYONE!

There *is* a condo for (almost) everyone! They are typically found in high-rise buildings in metropolitan areas and in lower-density levels in the suburbs. They are often found as dwellings in resort areas; even some hotels have been developed under a condominium ownership form. Condos may offer amenities to serve principally the market for young adults, families with young children, empty-nesters, or retirees. There are luxury condos and affordable condos. Commercial (office) condos have not caught on, however, perhaps because they offer few business advantages in comparison to fee simple ownership.

Condo ownership is easy to understand: Within a structure that contains a number of living units (generally apartments or town houses), you own your own unit, which you can mortgage, sell, or bequeath, and you have an undivided interest in the common areas. Cooperatives have not become as universally popular, perhaps because the ownership structure is more abstract, hence less well understood. Co-ops are found mostly in the New York City area, perhaps because a large portion of New Yorkers are comfortable with the concept of stock ownership.

It is remarkable that condos have caught on so quickly because overall trends in housing move at the speed of a glacier. The total number of housing units in the United States is 115 million. In a typical year, however, only about 1.5 million new housing units are built. That includes single-family homes, rental apartments, condos, and cooperatives. Mathematically, the annual supply of new housing units represents less than 1.5 percent of the available housing stock.

In the old days, two basic forms of homes predominated. One was the single-family home, typically detached. The other was the rental apartment. With notable exceptions in major cities, rental apartments were considered an inferior type of housing, to be used by those of low to moderate income levels, whereas the middle and upper-middle classes enjoyed home-ownership status.

In the 1950s some city dwellers in rental apartments found that they could capture the highly advantageous income tax deductions for mortgage interest and property taxes by buying a co-op or condo. Many buildings previously operated as rental units were converted to co-op or condo status, and existing tenants were offered the opportunity to purchase the units they were renting. Professional management was hired to maintain the buildings to the collective taste of the owner-occupants.

In the 1970s people all over the United States realized they could gain income tax benefits and also hedge against inflation by capturing the appreciation potential of real estate. Purchase of a condominium could potentially satisfy that requirement for their own housing needs, and a second unit to be used as a vacation home or rental property was also desirable. At that time, the stock and bond markets were both weak, and investors looked to tangibles such as real estate as a store of wealth and opportunity for gain.

Although some geographical areas became saturated with condos in the 1970s, especially with massive conversion of apartments to condos in some markets, and the market for condos plummeted, condo markets eventually stabilized in the 1980s and rebounded in the 1990s. As we begin to move through the new millennium, the recent experience with drastic market swings and the great moderation of inflation reduces the likelihood that market volatility will mirror the past.

2

WHAT IS A CONDOMINIUM?

There is a common misconception that a condominium, or condo for short, is a type of building. People refer to condos as if they represented a particular architectural style. Actually, condos can take many physical forms: high-rise apartments, garden-style apartments, town houses, even detached units. What distinguishes condos is the legal form of ownership. The condo is a legal innovation that allows you to enjoy property ownership within a complex that is shared with other people.

As a condo owner, you control your unit in the complex. Or to be more precise, you control the interior space of your unit. This allows you to take out a mortgage loan to purchase the unit and to obtain insurance to protect you from hazards and liability claims.

The remainder of the complex, including the exterior structure, grounds, and any improvements on the grounds, is owned in common with the other unit owners within the complex. You have the right to use and enjoy these components, but that right is constrained by the considerations for other owners' rights to equal use and enjoyment. This is like the right you have to use public streets while abiding by local laws and ordinances governing their use.

Control of the common areas in a condo is exercised by a condominium association. As an owner, you are automatically a member of the association and have a voice in the actions of the association. The association has a set of bylaws that determine what you are allowed to do in the common areas. The bylaws may even affect what you can do in your unit if those activities are likely to affect your neighbors. For example, you might not be able to keep a pet or use the unit for business purposes.

You are required to pay a periodic fee to the condo association to help support its activities. The fee pays for property maintenance and repairs to the common area, insurance, management fees, and utilities. Failure to pay this fee could result in a lien placed against your unit.

Despite the required fee, condo ownership is not maintenance-free. When you need work inside your unit, such as plumbing, painting, or an appliance repair, you arrange it and pay for it yourself. Sometimes the management company may suggest or even arrange for a reputable contractor, and the management company may bill you for the work so you won't have to deal with the contractor directly. Some people prefer to do their own maintenance work as it is often superior to the work a landlord would do; others prefer the predictability of lease rent and the freedom from repairs and maintenance.

Condo ownership mixes the advantages and disadvantages of home ownership with multifamily living. You may benefit from rising property values and income tax deductions but you must make a significant investment in your unit and you must find a buyer when you wish to move. You may be able to enjoy recreational facilities at lower cost but have limited control over your living environment. And, you must live close to other people. Some find this arrangement to be entirely satisfactory, while others discover it to be unpleasant.

3

WHAT IS A CO-OP?

Living in a co-op, or cooperative housing, is like living in an apartment and being your own landlord. You don't truly own the building or even the unit you live in, but you are a part owner of the building. The property is owned by a special purpose corporation. As a part owner, you hold stock in the corporation. The shares of stock provide the right to use an apartment in the building through a proprietary lease. Each unit is assigned a specified number of shares according to its size and desirability.

The building is owned by a corporation and the corporation is owned by its shareholders. The corporation may place a mortgage on the building and the corporation leases units in the building to the shareholders. All expenses connected with the building, including the mortgage payments, maintenance, taxes, and such, are paid by the shareholders in proportion to the number of shares owned. Ordinarily, an individual's tax deductions are figured without regard to stock he or she owns. However, special tax laws that apply to cooperatives create an exception to this rule. Individuals may deduct on their personal tax return their share of interest expense and the real estate taxes paid by the cooperative. This is an attractive aspect of cooperative ownership when compared to paying rent, a nondeductible expense to renters.

Shareholders also have a say in the operation of the building, although each individual shareholder must abide by the decision of the group. Portions of the property not covered by proprietary leases are common areas. These areas are not controlled by any one share-holder but are subject to common use and oversight. These common areas may include recreational facilities, passageways, and mechanical equipment such as elevators and heating plant.

Shareholders can borrow to purchase their shares, but the loan is not a mortgage loan. Rather, the co-op shares are used as collateral for the loan. The corporation probably has a mortgage loan on the entire building.

Shareholders can sell their shares and with them transfer the right to a proprietary lease. The corporation, however, may have the right to approve or disapprove the person to whom you sell the shares. As a share-holder, you may be able to sublease the unit, if allowed by the rules of the corporation. The rules of the corporation can be very strict and inclusive. They may cover all aspects of what you can do in your unit and how you may alter your unit. For this reason, familiarity with the rules of the corporation is important before committing to purchasing shares.

4

OWNERSHIP AND USE OF COMMON AREAS

In a condominium or co-op, everything other than the interior space of your unit, and the units of other owners, is considered common areas or elements. Since these areas or elements are shared in some way by more than one resident, your right to use these elements is limited by the bylaws of the association or co-op board. Likewise, your individual responsibility for maintaining these elements is limited. Let's take a look at what constitutes the common areas of a complex.

Structural elements of the building. These define the dimensions of your unit. You are constrained in the extent of alteration you can make to the walls, floors, and ceilings of your unit. Also, you are not responsible for making repairs to these elements (this may be relaxed in some smaller condominium complexes). The association will be concerned with anything that might violate the structural integrity of the building or that might affect pipes, wires, and ducts encased in the structure. You are also limited in how you can decorate the exterior surfaces. The concern here is mainly aesthetics and avoiding clashes of style and color. However, you may obtain permission for alterations from the association (for example, if you wish to install security equipment that does not interfere with your neighbors).

Exterior spaces. These areas are for the common use of residents. Included are lobbies, hallways, elevators, lawns, gardens, walkways, and drives. You will probably not be allowed to claim these areas for your exclusive use—even on a temporary basis—or be allowed to decorate them without special permission. Whether you are allowed to post signs, such as for sale signs or garage sale notices, is regulated by the bylaws.

Facilities. They may be provided for the use of residents. In larger complexes, there may be pools, sports courts, bike trails, and social centers. There is usually an established set of rules governing the use of these facilities, which may be available for private functions by reservation. Most conflicts among residents revolve around improvements to and expansion of these facilities, as the use and enjoyment of them is rarely shared equally among residents.

When selecting a place to buy, check the bylaws to try to get the mix of features that complements your lifestyle and see if you can live with the restrictions. Keep in mind that these restrictions apply to all owners, so they can protect you from certain behavior by others.

In general, the more elaborate the common areas, the higher your monthly fee will be. Trying to change the bylaws or lower the fees may be a difficult and futile venture, even if you yourself become a director of the association.

5

MANAGEMENT

In all co-ops and condos, there is an organization that oversees the common areas and handles any problems that may arise. In a co-op, this is the corporation. In a condo, it is the homeowners' association. When you buy a unit, you become a shareholder in the corporation or a member of the homeowners' association. This gives you a voice in how things are run.

To conduct the business of the organization, a smaller group of homeowners is vested with executive powers. In the co-op, this group is the Board of Directors. In a condo, it is the Executive or Operating Board. Either of these may be called simply "the board." Members of these groups are elected by the homeowners and usually serve on a voluntary basis. Membership is usually rotated among homeowners, so there is a good chance that you will someday serve as a board member.

Duties of the governing group. The main duties of the governing group are policy making and supervision. Very active boards or those in small complexes also enforce the bylaws and execute the budget of the organization. They will notify owners of violations of the bylaws and will be ready to bring action if necessary. They may handle disputes among owners even when these disputes are not covered by the bylaws. When there is no management company, one member will act as treasurer, prepare a budget, and see to it that money is spent as appropriated. The board is also in charge of collecting monthly fees to fund these operations.

Periodic meetings of owners are held to approve the budget, elect new officers, and vote on other matters. These meetings may be routine and uneventful or may

9

be acrimonious affairs where owner conflicts are brought into the open. It is up to the executive officers to make sure that conflicts are resolved and that actions reflect the majority opinion.

The Board of Directors of a co-op has an additional responsibility. It screens prospective owners and may approve or disapprove their application to move into the complex. The board's concern is that all prospective buyers are financially able to handle their share of the co-op expenses. In addition, it is concerned that buyers fit with other owners and not cause disruptions for them. There have been cases of wealthy and famous people being turned down by co-ops fearful of the noise or security problems they might cause for other residents. Co-ops are also leery of investors who are not interested in long-term residence in the building.

Meeting the board. Living in a co-op or condo is similar to being the resident of a small town. You are a voting member of the community with its own laws and a group established to enforce them. Selecting the right "community" is vital to enjoying your new home. If you are buying a co-op, you will be required to meet with the board prior to its approval of your application. Take the time to find out how things are run. In a condo, you may not meet the board, but it is worth the time to talk to the president of the homeowners' association prior to committing to purchase a unit.

What a homeowners' association can do and how it is accountable to individual owners are determined by state and local laws. That means that the rules vary significantly for different locations around the country. Before committing to a condo or co-op, you may want to get a copy of your state's condominium or cooperative statutes (these are often collected in one section of the law), as well as any local ordinances that pertain to these properties. These laws will tell you what types of reports the association is obligated to provide to owners and how disputes can be settled between owners or with the association.

6

BYLAWS

The importance of becoming familiar with the bylaws of a condominium or co-op before buying can't be overemphasized. (Bylaws may also be known as articles of organization, declarations of trust, or articles of association.) Whatever they are called, these rules and regulations will greatly determine how enjoyable life in your new home becomes. Consider the following hypothetical cases:

- The Andersons are avid gardeners. They find an attractive condo with an enclosed patio that is perfect for a small garden. After moving in, they discover that the bylaws strictly limit the type of plants that can be grown due to allergy problems of many of their neighbors.
- The Browns buy into a co-op building. They plan to spend the summer in Europe and would like to sublet their unit while they are gone. To their dismay, they find that the bylaws do not allow this type of arrangement.

In addition to these restrictions, the bylaws may prevent owners from making unauthorized alterations, keeping pets, and using units for business purposes. The hours for using recreational facilities may be limited. In many cases, condo and co-op owners may feel more like rental tenants than owner-occupants.

Co-op rules are generally more restrictive and comprehensive than those for condos. In a co-op you really are a tenant, whereas in a condo you own the interior space. Therefore, co-op rules may cover much of what you are allowed to do within the interior of your unit. In addition, the co-op board has the authority to approve prospective residents.

You may wonder why anyone would put up with these restrictions. Remember that the bylaws were created by the residents of the complex. They are not meant to be punitive, but are designed to make the sharing of space by various households work to the satisfaction of all concerned. If a rule does not express the wishes of the majority of residents, it can be changed. However, don't expect to change the rules *after* you move in. Assume that the majority likes things the way they are and consider how well you can live with the rules before you commit to buy. You may find that the rules are helpful when they prevent your neighbors from doing something that you find offensive.

Enforcing the rules. Don't be misled by lax enforcement of the rules. Because a rule is not enforced doesn't mean it will not affect you. Residents have the power to sue for enforcement of the rules in many states. However, if you agree with the rules, but they are not being enforced, you may want to choose another complex that is more conscientious.

In addition to the rules and regulations, the bylaws have other functions.

1. They establish the government of the complex (we mentioned earlier that co-ops and condos are like miniature communities).
2. They describe the duties of the board or association officers, how they are chosen, how long they serve, and whether they are paid.
3. Rules for owner meetings and the conduct of business are included. They set procedures for establishing fees and how they are collected.

One of the reasons people are drawn to condominiums, or even subdivisions with strong homeowners' associations, is the orderly and tidy appearance provided by a good set of bylaws and a diligent owners' association. However, if something you like is prohibited, your enjoyment of your property will be diminished. Some condo associations do prohibit pets, even when they are well behaved and kept on a leash. In at least one state, an association can prevent homeowners from smoking even in their units. And a not uncommon authority retained by associations is the right to approve unit sales or the right of first refusal when a unit is put on the market. If the unit you are considering has this feature, find out if local lenders will make a loan on the unit. Clearly, examination of all the documents governing the condo and association is as important as physically inspecting the unit.

7

CONDOMINIUMS AND CO-OPS AS INVESTMENTS

The concept of condominium and cooperative housing was developed to give more people a chance to own their homes. However, many people own units that they rent out to others rather than live there themselves. For these people, the condo or co-op is purely an investment.

There are six major reasons why someone might invest in these units:

1. Real estate offers an excellent way to diversify assets, especially for someone who is heavily in the stock or bond markets. Prices of some real estate have run counter to stock and bond fluctuations, providing a perfect diversification vehicle. Many want to buy real estate but do not understand the market or know how values are estimated; thus they are afraid of being swindled. For these, a condo or co-op at or near their own home provides peace of mind. A condo is something that most people understand, even when they are not knowledgeable investors.

2. Most real estate offers a hedge against inflation, although there may be local economic variations that offset this effect. An investor who is concerned about inflation should seriously consider including real estate in a portfolio.

3. An investor may take advantage of a depressed market to buy a unit for a good price. On the other hand, an occupant-owner may give up trying to

sell in a down market and convert the unit into a rental unit. Under normal conditions, buying a condo or co-op costs more than a comparable rental unit would, so it may require a market downturn to make buying condos or co-ops feasible as an investment.

4. Operating one unit allows you to be a real estate investor on a limited scale. This may be a good way to break in to rental housing without overextending your finances and time. In contrast to a detached rental home, operating a rental condo or co-op frees you from many of the property management tasks.

5. The market for rental housing may be better than that for owner-occupied homes. In addition, a condo or co-op may be able to command a higher rent than a comparable unit in an all-rental complex.

6. When a building is first converted into a condo or co-op, there may be several units that remain rentals because the occupants don't want to buy and the converter can't evict them, either as a legal or practical matter. You may be able to buy these units at a good price and maintain them as rentals. You also have the advantage of a rented-out unit.

Taxable income generated. You will have to do some special accounting to calculate the taxable income generated by the investment. From the sum of all rental receipts you collect during the year, you can deduct all ordinary and necessary expenses connected with operating the property. These include utility bills you paid, maintenance or condo fees, insurance, property taxes, and repairs. Major improvements and replacement of large components cannot be deducted but are added to the basis of the property, then depreciated. Further, you can deduct the interest you pay on the mortgage loan (in the case of a co-op, include your share of the co-op's loan as well as the loan used to buy your shares) and an amount for depreciation of the building. For residential property, you are allowed a depreciation deduction of 3.64 percent of the value of the unit each year. The amount, after taking out interest and depreciation, is your taxable income from the property.

Possible losses. If a loss occurs, it may be used to off-set other income, provided the loss is under $25,000, you make important decisions on leasing the property, you approve major expenses, and your taxable income is under $100,000 without subtracting your loss from this property. If your income exceeds $100,000, but is less than $150,000, you may still use the loss, but the $25,000 limit is reduced by 50 cents for every dollar that your taxable income exceeds $100,000. However, if you fail to meet these conditions, this passive loss cannot be used to offset your salary (active) or interest and divi-dend (portfolio) income.

Checking the bylaws. Before planning to use a condo or co-op unit as an investment, you need to check the bylaws or lease to see if renting out units is allowed. If so, you should know if any special restrictions apply, such as getting approval of your tenant from the board. Because of restrictions, running a co-op as a rental unit is often not practical.

Financing. Check on financing before getting too far along in your plans. Mortgage loans for condos for absentee owners are harder to find and/or are more expensive than owner-occupant financing. If you live in the condo and plan to convert it to a rental, you need not inform the lender but may retain the old loan. This can save you some expense on financing. You should not get a loan under the pretense of living in the unit if you do not intend to do so. You may be prosecuted for fraud.

8

VACATION CONDOS

In the minds of many, a condo on the beach or in the mountains is the epitome of luxury living. Besides the status of owning such a property, there may be advantages in knowing you have a retreat available when you need it. Furthermore, such opportunities are open for those with something less than luxury incomes.

There are several ways you can control a vacation condo. The most straightforward method is simply to buy a condo unit in some desirable resort area. Unless you plan to use the unit every weekend, you can rent it out when you are not using it. Some resort condos offer rental management services to owners for a fee. In general, you are responsible for getting tenants and setting the rent schedule.

Timeshares. Alternatively, you can buy an interest in a resort condo for a certain period of time each year. These "timeshares" give you the right to use the property during your designated time. The rest of the year is sold to other timeshare owners. Further, you may buy an actual timeshare interest in the property or acquire the right to use the property only. In the former case, you receive title to a piece of the unit representing your proportional share of the year. You can sell this interest in the market, give it away, or leave it to your heirs. When you buy a right to use the property, you don't have real property. However, if your right is in the form of a license, you can sell the right on the market. In addition, a right to use may have a limited life, whereas real property ownership is indefinite. Timeshares are versatile. The concept has been applied to cruise ships, houseboats, campsites, and recreational vehicles, as well as resort condos.

The advantages of owning a vacation condo (or timeshare) are the predictability of the expense and having a voice in how the property is run. Fixing the future cost of vacations is a prime selling point in most resort condos and timeshares. However, you should be aware that a source of future cost increases is the annual fee you pay for maintenance. All you have fixed is the purchase cost of the unit or timeshare.

The two principal disadvantages are that you are limited to spending your vacation at the same place (and, in the case of timeshares, at the same time) each year, and your investment is illiquid. The problem of going to the same place each year can be alleviated through exchange networks where owners can temporarily trade places. To best use the network, you should have a place that has broad appeal. Don't expect to trade a week in August at a Louisiana fishing lake for a winter week in Hawaii. Your ability to trade up in an exchange depends on how the organization handling the exchange rates the desirability of your unit and the time of year you own. Unless your unit is located in a highly desirable area and has substantial amenities, you probably should regard the right to exchange as adding little value, and adjust your offer price accordingly.

Your ability to sell your condo or timeshare may be severely limited. First, the market for your property may be thin, depending on the economic conditions, the availability of financing, and the attractiveness of the property. Recognize that the resale market for vacation condos and timeshares is not as well organized as for homes. Second, if you own a timeshare right to use, you may not have anything to sell. If you are buying partially as an investment, you must find out whether you can legally sell your interest. The title to your timeshare or use right may not be transferable. In some cases, your interest reverts to the developer if you decide to terminate your participation. This is a good thing to determine before you buy.

Should you own your vacation condo in fee simple or buy a timeshare? If you buy the property, you will probably have to make a larger investment and will need bank financing. However, you are in the relatively secure position of having title to the property. You may be able to sell later for a profit and can deduct some expenses from your taxes, depending on whether you rent the place out. A timeshare will require a smaller investment, although you cannot generate rental income, and it is much less complicated. You don't have to solicit tenants for the time you're not using the place. You have more limited resale opportunities and your use of the property is more limited.

Whether you have a title or simple right to use, your interest in the property is tied to the success of the endeavor and the viability of the developer-owner. If the project goes under or the developer runs into problems, your investment may evaporate. Key 46 provides tax information for people who own second and vacation homes.

Promotions. Resort condos and especially time-shares are often sold through special promotions in which prospective buyers are given incentives to visit the property. Quite often, people in nearby states are offered "free" vacations in conjunction with the visit. Many times, people who agree to these promotions are subjected to high-pressure sales tactics in an effort to induce a quick sale.

You may take such an approach as a sign that the project is not a good value. However, regardless of the way the project is promoted, you should not let the sales pitch prevent you from gathering the information essential to making an informed decision. You may want to find out more about the area before visiting. While at the development, evaluate the facilities without input from the salespeople. If any facility is promised but not yet completed, consider how enjoyable the place would be without that facility. Finally, ask the local Better Business Bureau for a reliability report on the developer.

And the free vacation or prize offer? Before you accept, find out what your part of the expenses will be. It may be that the prize is not worth the cost.

Timeshares and timeshare promotions are not regulated through federal law. However, various states do require promoters to abide by prescribed procedures. You may want to contact the state government where the development is located and find out what your legal rights are in regard to these promotions.

9

AFFORDABILITY AND LOAN QUALIFYING

A good place to start when considering buying a home is to figure out how expensive a home you can afford. This will depend on your income and how much money you have available for a down payment. Your income determines how large a loan you will be able to get. The available down payment can then be added to the loan amount to get to the price.

Qualifying. Mortgage lenders determine how large a loan you will get through a process called *qualifying*. The purpose of qualifying is to estimate the likelihood that you will make timely loan payments. Therefore, the process places great importance on your income, your debt obligations aside from the mortgage, and your past credit history.

You may simulate the lender's qualifying process to get an idea of the size of the loan you can get and the price range of homes you can afford.

1. Estimate your income. Your may include both your salary or wages and that of your spouse, income from investments, and any support payments you receive. The key is to include only income from sources that are regular and consistent. This includes part-time jobs that are permanent, but not income from temporary jobs, special bonuses, and one-time investment gains. If you are self-employed or on commission, you should use an average of the past several years' income.

2. Calculate how much of your income can be applied toward mortgage payments. If you get a fixed-rate loan, lenders often allow up to 33 percent of gross income for monthly payments of interest, principal, taxes, and insurance, and up to 38 percent to cover these expenses plus other debt payments. (The ratios are 28 and 36 percent if you need a mortgage for over 90 percent of the house's value.) Divide your monthly income amount by 3 to get your maximum allowable monthly payment. If your monthly debt payments, other than mortgage, are less that 5 percent of monthly income, you can use the 33 percent amount for qualifying. However, if your debts are more, you must use the 38 percent amount (multiply your income by .38 and subtract your monthly debt payments).

Add the amount of down payment you can make to the loan amount. But don't apply all your cash to the down payment. Retain some cash for other expenses associated with purchase—most homeowners want new curtains, wallpaper, paint, lawn and garden supplies, tools, and equipment. If possible, retain at least 3 or 4 percent of the loan amount. The total of the loan and down payment is the maximum-priced home you can afford. Divide the price by the loan amount. If the ratio is 80 percent or less, you can get a standard loan. If not, you will need an insured or FHA loan. The qualifying ratios for these types of loans are less generous than the ones you used, so you will have to scale back your maximum price a bit.

The following table gives an approximation of the home price affordability as a multiple of your gross income. It is based on a 90 percent loan-to-value ratio. To use the table, first find the interest rate you can borrow at in the column on the left. Across the top find an estimate of taxes and insurance as a percentage of housing prices. The factor at their intersection gives the multiple of earnings you can afford. For example, suppose mortgage interest rates are 8 percent and property taxes and insurance combined are approximately 3 percent of the property value; your annual gross income is $60,000. You can afford a house of about 3.0 times your gross income, or $180,000.

Home Affordability Limits (Estimated) as a Multiple of Gross Income

Interest Rate	Property Taxes and Insurance as Percent of Price				
	1	2	3	4	5
7.0%	4.0	3.6	3.2	3.0	2.7
7.5	3.9	3.5	3.1	2.9	2.6
8.0	3.7	3.3	3.0	2.8	2.6
8.5	3.5	3.2	2.9	2.7	2.5
9.0	3.4	3.1	2.8	2.6	2.4
9.5	3.3	3.0	2.7	2.5	2.3
10.0	3.1	2.9	2.6	2.4	2.3
10.5	3.0	2.8	2.6	2.4	2.2
11.0	2.9	2.7	2.5	2.3	2.2
11.5	2.8	2.6	2.4	2.2	2.1
12.0	2.7	2.5	2.3	2.2	2.0

Your estimate is not intended to be highly accurate, but you don't need a precise figure at this stage. What you want is a ballpark figure to begin your decision process and market search. This bit of analysis should help you start and prevent disappointment from finding your dream house and discovering it is out of reach.

Preapprovals. If you do not want to make these calculations yourself, contact a lender and ask to be "prequalified." The lender will ask you a few questions about your income and estimate how large a loan that income would support. Being prequalified does not obligate you to take out a loan from that lender, nor does it obligate the lender to give you a loan. It merely provides you with information so that you can do a more focused job of finding a home. Some people may take the further step of getting "preapproved" for a loan. This procedure may involve a fee and additional information about your financial position, including getting your credit report. If you are uncertain about your ability to get a loan, however, preapproval may be worth the cost.

10

OWNING VERSUS RENTING

Although living in a co-op or condo may seem to be similar to living in a rental apartment, the commitment of owning your own home is much different. There are distinct advantages and disadvantages to owning a home. The first step in evaluating whether to buy a home is deciding if home ownership is for you.

Advantages of owning

Home ownership is the aspiration of many families. Almost two-thirds of Americans own their own home. There are a number of advantages they enjoy:

- *Pride of ownership.* Many people take comfort in a place they can call their own. Owning your home may make you feel more at home than occupying someone else's property.
- *Status.* As a homeowner, you may feel more respected as a stable member of the community. You may also find it easier to arrange credit and do other things where trustworthiness is required.
- *Autonomy.* As an owner, you have more freedom to alter the property to your own tastes than as a renter; however, your ability to make alterations to a co-op/condo may be highly restricted. Furthermore, any improvements made are yours to keep rather than becoming the property of the landlord. You also have the security of knowing that your tenure is not limited by the term of your current lease. As long as you meet your financial obligations relative to the property, you can't be evicted.

- *Variety.* Buying a home may provide you with more options in the type of home and location. In most cases, the rental housing market is more limited than homes for sale. If you are looking for a certain type of home or a particular neighborhood, you may have to buy.
- *Tax advantages.* The money you spend on mortgage interest and property taxes is deductible from your taxable income. This can lower the actual cost of buying a home. However, recent tax changes have reduced the value of these benefits. Check with your tax advisor to see if owning a home is to your advantage tax-wise.
- *Appreciation.* Hopefully, the value of the home you buy will increase over time, although this is not always the case. If you have selected a quality home and not paid more than its market value, you may have a good investment. When you buy with a mortgage loan, the return on your cash investment can be greater than the rate at which the property value increases.

Advantages of renting
Renting has its advantages as well. Before you decide to buy, consider these points:

- *Mobility.* If you are not ready to commit to an area, a neighborhood, or a particular house, you may want to rent. When you own your home, you must find another buyer when you want to move. This will take time and, usually, cost money for transaction costs such as brokerage commissions. If the market is slow, you may have great difficulty making a sale and may end up losing some of your investment.
- *Liquidity.* Buying a home requires the investment of a considerable amount of money. Often, a home makes up the large majority of a family's wealth. If the need for money arises, it is often hard to convert

this investment to cash, although the recent innovation of home equity loans makes this less of a problem. The renter may keep his or her money in the bank or have other investments that are liquid.

- *Liability.* Owning a home can be a big responsibility. The renter is relieved of much of this responsibility by the landlord. The renter generally does not have to pay for repairs or maintenance and may have less liability for lawsuits in case someone is injured on the property, unless it is due to the negligence of the renter.
- *Lower costs.* It is often the case that out-of-pocket costs are lower for renting a comparable home than for buying. Some of this is because of the tax benefits of owning, but much is due to people's preference for owning. If you wish to limit your immediate expenditures for housing, you probably will want to rent.

11

MULTIFAMILY VERSUS SINGLE-FAMILY

The biggest difference between living in a single-family, detached home and in a condo or co-op is the close proximity of your neighbors. When you live in a detached home, you have a buffer of lawn, and maybe a fence, between you and your neighbor. In a condo or co-op, this division is often no more than a common wall. In addition, once you are outside your unit, you are sharing space with the other residents. One of the most important considerations in buying a condo or co-op is deciding whether this type of living arrangement is suitable for you and your family.

Condo/co-op living does have certain advantages. Among them are the following.

Cost. Multifamily housing uses less land and is often more economical to build because of common structural components and other design features. Therefore, these units are generally less expensive than detached homes of similar size and quality (of course, condo/co-ops can be very expensive housing when placed in exclusive locations, such as Park Avenue in New York City). Lower-priced units are good starter homes for first-time home buyers. Lower prices also mean smaller loan amounts, making it easier for young families to qualify for a mortgage. Attached units may also be less expensive to heat and cool because of the insulating effect of neighboring units.

Location. Because they take less land per unit,

condo/co-ops can be developed on high-cost land within major cities. This appeals to some people, as they like being closer to downtown job and entertainment centers. On the other hand, these locations may not be as residential in character as single-family neighborhoods. Therefore, this is a judgment you must make based on your desired lifestyle.

Low maintenance. A big attraction to some condo/co-op residents is the freedom from many of the routine household tasks. Generally, such things as lawn maintenance and outside repairs are the responsibility of the association or board. You pay for these services through your monthly fee. However, this is often cheaper than contracting independently for these services.

Lifestyle. Some complexes are designed to promote certain lifestyles. There may be organized social functions for young single adults. Some older single people may like the security of having neighbors close by. Elaborate common area facilities may be conducive to entertaining. However, many complexes are not amenable to residents with small children or pets, or those who like gardening.

There are several disadvantages of living in attached housing, which is why some people would not be happy living in a condo or co-op. If the following concerns bother you, you should consider an alternative to buying a condo/co-op:

- *Privacy.* This is probably the biggest objection many people have to condos and co-ops. Good design can minimize this problem. Soundproofing in common walls and ceilings, private entryways (often associated with town house designs), and private patios and decks can reduce the intrusion of your neighbors. However, attached housing always involves some loss of privacy.
- *Control.* Much of what you can do in your home is determined by the bylaws of the condo/co-op and majority rule of the owners' association or corpo-

ration. If you cherish the independence that home ownership entails, you may not want to own a condo or co-op.

- *Status.* To many, condos and co-ops are indistinguishable from rental apartments. Therefore, you may find that much of the status advantage normally attached to home ownership is lost when you own a condo or co-op. In some areas, mortgage financing for these units has been a problem. Lenders either are unfamiliar with condo/co-op ownership or feel that the units are not as marketable, and therefore less valuable collateral, as detached homes.

- *Appreciation.* Markets for condos have been less stable than those for detached homes. In some areas, builders have badly overestimated the market and a surplus of condos exists. Then too, if demand for condos increases, rental apartments can be converted quickly to increase the supply. This means that the value of your unit may not increase as rapidly as other types of housing.

- *Resale restrictions.* For co-ops, the authority of the board to screen prospective tenants may complicate your ability to sell your unit for the best price. By contrast, condo sales may generally be effected without neighbors' approval.

12

CHOOSING BETWEEN A CONDO AND A CO-OP

If you have decided that multifamily home ownership is for you, you have the choice of a condo or co-op. Actually, much of this choice is dictated by where you live. Co-ops are common in New York City and some other large cities, but are sparse elsewhere. Condos are found in almost all cities. However, there is the chance that you may face choosing between the two types of housing.

The differences between a condo a co-op are not readily obvious. There is nothing in the way they look or how people live in them that distinguishes condos from co-ops. What does set these two apart is the legal basis of ownership, and that can make a significant difference in how well one or the other fits your situation.

When you buy a condo, you actually own real property. The internal space of your unit is yours outright, while you have an undivided interest in everything else in the complex. In a co-op, you are a shareholder in a corporation that owns the complex. As a shareholder you are entitled to a lease giving you the right to occupy a unit. However, you are essentially a tenant in the building, although your lease doesn't have an expiration date and you have a voice in how the place is run.

There are other differences that stem from this distinction in ownership.

1. Your ability to decorate and alter even the interior of your unit is more restricted in a co-op. In a condo, you can do most anything you want to the

interior that doesn't affect the structure or interfere with your neighbors.

2. When you buy into a co-op, you must gain approval from the board. Likewise, the board must approve your sale. By contrast, you can buy and sell a condo unit just as you would a detached home.

3. You can't get a true mortgage loan to buy into a co-op. To finance purchase of your shares, you will need to use your stock as collateral for the loan. Interest paid on this loan is still tax-deductible since it is a loan for the purpose of obtaining your principal residence. On the other hand, it shouldn't cost as much to buy a co-op share as it would to buy a condo unit.

4. As a co-op owner, you will pay maintenance fees, which may include interest and principal payments on a master mortgage loan used to purchase the building. In fact, many of the direct expenses you would have in a condo, such as mortgage payments, property taxes, and homeowners' insurance, are paid for indirectly through fees to the co-op board. To make tax deductions for eligible expenses, you will get a prorated list for each apartment from the board or an amount to deduct per share.

In a co-op, many of the aspects of multifamily living described in the previous Key are extended. Condo ownership is closer to the situation of a single-family home. Therefore, if the considerations of multifamily life cause you some concern, you would probably be happier in a condo than in a co-op.

13

CONDO-/CO-OP-BUYING PROCESS

If you are a first-time condo or co-op buyer, you may be unfamiliar with the steps required to buy. The procedure can be complicated. However, considering that you are choosing the place in which you will live for some time, and probably making the largest investment of your life, you might expect buying to involve some time and effort. A real estate sales agent can help guide you through the procedure, and you may engage the services of an attorney to assist with the contracts. Nevertheless, it is a good idea to understand what is expected so you can be prepared to move the process along.

Obviously, the first step is to find the place where you want to buy. Before looking at condos or co-ops, try to get an idea of what you want. Read the Keys discussing the differences in owning and renting, single-family versus multifamily housing, and condominiums versus co-ops. Consider what you need in space and features and in what part of town you would like to locate. Finally, determine the price range of condo or co-op you can afford (Key 9).

Once you have an idea of what you are looking for, you can make a more effective search of the market. You may respond to ads from sellers or contact a sales agent. The agent can show you a wide range of homes in a relatively short period of time. You may want to secure a broker who will work for you. See the next Key, A Buyer's Broker, for more information on brokers.

The offer. When you have found the place that suits your needs, you should make an offer. This will take the form of a binder or a formal sales contract stating the price you wish to pay and any conditions on the sale. The seller will consider the offer and either accept it, reject it, or make a counteroffer. If the seller counters, you may agree or make another offer. This negotiation will continue until either side terminates negotiations or both sides agree. When you and the seller sign the sales contract, the sale is complete—subject to any contingencies listed in the contract.

A counteroffer is legally a rejection of the offer and a simultaneous substitution of a new offer. The slightest change to an offer constitutes a complete rejection of the entire offer.

The contract. The contract sets a date for the closing, a time when legal title to the home is officially transferred. In the meantime, you must arrange financing. This involves contacting a mortgage lender—unless the seller is providing the financing—and applying for a loan. After you make a formal application, the lender needs some time to determine if the loan can be granted. This may require several weeks, during which the unit will be appraised, your credit history will be reviewed, and information you provided will be verified. If the loan is approved, the lender will give you a commitment to provide the funds at the closing.

The closing. While the loan is being processed, you will want to prepare for the closing. This may include having a professional inspect the house, ordering a survey to be conducted, and arranging insurance. The seller will fix any problems found (if agreed to in the contract) and have a lawyer prepare the deed to be transferred. At the closing, all fees and payments are distributed to the parties involved and you become the new owner of the home. All that remains is moving in.

14

A BUYER'S BROKER

Historically, the seller arranged for a broker to represent him or her using a listing agreement. The buyer often found a broker who was paid a share of the commission by the seller's broker, who worked under the listing agreement and thus legally worked for the seller.

In the 1990s, a trend developed whereby a broker—or agent working under a broker—works for a buyer. This is disclosed to all parties in a document called *agency disclosure*. Frequently, the seller pays a full commission, compensating both his or her own listing broker and the buyer's broker. Still, the buyer's broker's commitment is to get the best deal for the buyer, not the seller.

Some brokers represent either buyers or sellers, depending on who contacts them. Other brokers represent only buyers and are practiced in the art of being a champion of the buyer's cause.

Some things to consider in selecting a broker to assist a potential buyer in a purchase are

1. Can the broker provide complete loyalty?
2. Is the broker knowledgeable and active in the market being considered?
3. Is the broker a full-time and experienced broker?
4. Are there any limitations the broker or his or her firm may have in representing the buyer or any conflicts the broker or his or her firm may have with representing sellers?
5. What experience, skill, and training does the broker have in negotiating for a buyer?
6. Is the broker experienced in presenting offers?
7. Does the broker have access to market data infor-

mation, including recent sales and property currently on the market?

8. Does the broker have contacts with and/or standing arrangements for other services?
   - Home inspectors
   - Environmental inspectors
   - Attorneys
   - Title companies
   - Providers of financing

It is important to work with a buyer's broker who understands your situation, particularly the timing of your purchase. When you need to move into a condo or co-op by August 20 so your children can start school in their new district, you don't want your broker to specify requirements that are deal killers. The broker may think he or she is working to get you the best price or contract terms, when you would gladly accept something less in exchange for a timely settlement.

Under different circumstances, price may be critical to your interest. You may be willing to risk losing out on a particular home if the owner won't accept your price. Make your intentions clear to the broker to minimize the chance of killing the deal you want.

It may be more important for you to get your terms—unit condition, move-in date, contingencies—in a contract than to get the best possible price. If you are trying to do both—get your price *and* your terms—you may be pushing the limits of negotiations to the point where your offer is unacceptable.

15

THE INTERNET

The World Wide Web is a fertile source of information about real estate. An informative first step is to visit the web site of the National Association of REALTORS®, *www.realtor.com*. This will provide information to help find a house, condo, or co-op, a neighborhood, a REALTOR®, or a lender.

From there, determine whether the local board of REALTORS® or MLS has a web site to tell about its members and dwelling units for sale. Check sites of local REALTORS® and brokers. Some other useful sites are Microsoft's *www.homeadvisor.com* (for finding both homes and loans) and *www.homeshark.com*. The International Real Estate Directory also has a highly useful site at *www.ired.com*. Available houses can be found through *www.homeseekers.com*.

The direction and speed of the growth of the Internet will soon lead to a national market for houses and loans. It won't be long before every house that is listed for sale with a REALTOR® will be on the 'Net. Data will include a photo, floor plan, and specifications, such as lot size, size of the dwelling, room size, age, school district, etc. You will simply choose your price range and location of interest, by city and state or ZIP code, to obtain a preview list. If the list includes more dwellings offered than you can visit, you can narrow the search parameters; if it offers too few dwellings, you can widen the search.

In the not-too-distant future we may also see offerings of condos and co-ops that are sold without a broker, with a similar search mechanism. An owner puts a condo or co-op on the market through the Web by paying a small fee and providing the necessary data. Interested buyers can visit and inspect the dwelling. The next step might be a downloadable contract, or even an on-line form, where you would just fill in the blanks to make an offer. The proposed contract could be e-mailed to your attorney for review and a final contract e-mailed to the lender and title company. The lender may receive your credit report and hazard insurance binder by e-mail. An AVM (automated valuation model) appraisal, using local statistical data, can be procured quickly at a low cost. You may find a lender on the 'Net either by going to the specific sites for various lenders or by visiting a site that provides a list of lenders, loan types, and rates that are updated daily.

As for information on loans available today (in 2000), you can visit the sites of FNMA, FHLMC, the VA, and FHA/HUD to get a feel for mortgage types and availability, as well as current qualifying requirements. These addresses are

www.fanniemae.com

www.freddiemac.com and *www.homesteps.com* (Freddie Mac's site for available houses)

www.va.gov and *www.vba.va.gov* (Veterans Benefits Administration)

www.hud.gov/lenders1.html and

www.hud.gov/broker1.html (information on FHA lenders and brokers of dwellings subject to FHA loans)

National mortgage brokers and other lenders have web sites. Some sites simply describe the loans and terms, while others will take an application over the phone. Countrywide (*www.countrywide.com*) and The Associates (*www.theassociates.com*) are two national lenders.

Some buyers have access to organizations that offer especially good rates. For example, *www.usaa.com* and *www.navyfcu.org* are for former military personnel.

Keep in mind that almost anyone can go into real estate or mortgage lending and set up a web site. The presence of a web site is not a substitute for a good referral or a good deal.

16

PITFALLS WHEN BUYING

If you are seriously considering a condo or co-op unit, you may have to do a bit more investigative work than you would when buying a detached home. It's not enough to determine that you like the unit and its location. More than just a place to live, condominium or cooperative housing carries the responsibility of joining a group of other homeowners in a financial partnership. It's even more complicated when a developer or converter is involved.

What this means is that there are more potential pitfalls in buying condos and co-ops. You must investigate by observing how the complex operates and critically examining the legal documents.

The documents are important but don't assume the whole story is presented there. In many cases, these documents were prepared long ago and have not been updated to reflect recent changes. There may be rules that have been enacted more recently that are not written into the bylaws or the "boilerplate" of the proprietary lease. The courts have ruled that such unwritten rules can be enforced. Find out if such rules exist and what they are.

On the other hand, there may be rules and obligations of the association or operating board printed in the documents but not followed. The board may have found them impractical or too expensive and dropped them with the acquiescence of the residents. If there are things you think are important, ask existing residents or officers if they are still in force.

Knowing association costs. You should be aware of things that may cost you more money than you anticipate. Let's say you are buying a condo unit and find out that the monthly fee is $150. You decide this amount can fit into your budget. After buying, you discover that the previous owner was paying $100 a month on a note for replacing the roof. Without realizing it, you assumed that note in the transaction. You then find out that an impending lawsuit against the association was settled and each member must pay out $500 in the settlement. Finally, you see that the association is not carrying liability insurance on the building and you must provide your own policy at a cost of $400 a year. Beware of these hidden costs. One suggestion is to require the seller to disclose—in the contract—such costs. If the seller omits or misrepresents, he or she would be liable.

Knowledge of unsold units. Try to find out who owns the other units in the development. If it is relatively new, the developer may still own most of them. If the units are selling, this may be no problem, but if a large number of developer-owned units persists, the developer can use its position to make the owners' association go along with things favorable to the developer but not so good for the owners. In an older development, the same type of problem—control by few people—may occur if few investors own enough units to control the owners' association; each owner gets a vote for each unit owned.

The basic problem is not so much multiple ownership as it is absentee ownership, since the owner's decisions may not coincide with the interests of those who live in the development.

Other problems could emerge if many of the units are occupied by renters. Most often, renter-occupants do not have the same interests as owner-occupants and may not be as diligent about upkeep. In addition, some mortgage lenders may be unwilling to finance the purchase of units in a development where too many units are rented.

Knowing special laws. Some states and cities have special laws that provide some protection for buyers of condos, co-ops, or resort timeshares. Check to see if there are any such laws in your area. In most cases, these laws require the seller to provide certain disclosures or documents before you have to commit to a purchase. They may also give you a certain amount of time to change your mind after agreeing to buy. Knowing your rights as a buyer can help you reach a more sensible decision.

17

CO-OP CHECKLIST

As you search the market for a co-op unit, consider the following items. You may use these points to eliminate specific units from consideration or to compare different units on the market.

- *Price.* How does the asking price compare to other co-op units, other comparable condominium units, and other alternative housing of any type?
- *Maintenance fee.* Consider the fee in relation to what is included. Does it include liability insurance or must you provide additional insurance? How much of the fee is deductible for tax purposes (mortgage interest and property taxes)?
- *Parking.* What provision is made for car storage and protection? Is there an additional fee for parking? Is a garage available?
- *Storage.* Is there a provision for storage outside of the unit? Is it secure? How much room is provided?
- *Facilities.* Are there recreational and entertaining facilities? What facilities are important to you?
- *Lifestyle.* Is the building designed to accommodate the way you prefer to live? How well would you fit in with the group currently living there?
- *Ownership.* Will your ownership interest be considered real or personal property according to state law? Can you finance the purchase with a mortgage loan?
- *Approval.* Must you submit to an interview before you are allowed to purchase shares? How extensive is the interview?

- *Location.* Is the unit convenient to your place of work or other areas of interest to you? Is the neighborhood desirable to you as a place to live?
- *Style.* Is the unit attractive? Is adequate privacy provided? Do you have a private entrance to your unit? Is adequate soundproofing provided between units?
- *Utilities.* What types of utilities are available? Do these accommodate your needs?
- *Budget.* Is the corporation carrying a heavy debt load relative to the value of the building? Are adequate reserves held? How are special needs financed?
- *Condition.* Is the building in good shape? Can you hire a qualified inspector to check out the unit and the building?
- *Bylaws.* What alterations are allowed? Are pets allowed? Can you sublease the unit (who gets to keep the rent)? What activities are prohibited? What type of insurance is required? Does the corporation have right of first refusal when a unit is placed up for sale?
- *Lease.* What special provisions are required in the proprietary lease? Are there additional restrictions on what you can do in or to your unit?
- *Financing.* Financing the purchase of your co-op shares can be a problem. Special financing may be available from specialized co-op share lenders. Before you can get such a loan, the co-op must be approved by the lender, so you should find out if such approval has been arranged.
- *Control.* Are several units owned by an investor who controls many votes? Or is ownership and voting control widely dispersed?

18

CONDO CHECKLIST

If you have decided that a condominium is suitable, here is a list of considerations to use during your house-hunting chore.

- *Attraction.* Condos are attractive for at least one of several reasons: location, amenities, or price. You should understand which of these is the main attraction of the unit under consideration. This will help you select the right unit as well as assist you when it is time to sell.
- *Style.* The most common types of condos are high-rise buildings, garden-style apartments, and town houses. Of these types, town houses are generally the most attractive to a broad range of buyers. High-rise units are usually luxury condos located near downtown. Style can determine how well the unit maintains its value in the market.
- *Conversions.* Was the complex rental apartments that were converted to condominiums? How successful was the conversion? Are some units reverting to rental? Is the converter still involved with the project?
- *New construction.* Does the developer still own a substantial number of units? Are the facilities complete?
- *Resident mix.* How many units are occupied by rental tenants? Renters and owners often have different attitudes about property upkeep that may lead to conflict. If too high a percentage of units are rented, you may have trouble getting mortgage financing.

- *Monthly fee.* How much is the monthly association fee? Has it been rising sharply in recent years? Are emergencies funded by assessing the owners or is a substantial reserve fund maintained?
- *Hidden fees.* Are common areas owned by the condominium or are there ground leases involved? These leases may be a source of rising costs in the future. Are there long-term management contracts entered into by the original developer? Such contracts may lead to complacency by hired management that may be hard to replace.
- *Financing.* Financing is more readily available if the complex has been approved by the FHA and FNMA. Points to be considered include the following: Does the seller have an assumable mortgage loan? Is the seller willing to sell with an FHA or VA loan? Is seller financing available? These issues are more important when mortgage interest rates are high. Before purchasing, check with local lenders to find out if mortgage financing is available. In some depressed markets, financing for condos has disappeared.
- *Other items.* See the checklist for co-ops. Specifically, check the following items.

Price	Parking	Storage
Facilities	Lifestyle	Location
Utilities	Condition	Rules

19

MAKING AN OFFER

When you have found a condo or co-op that you feel is suitable, you are ready to make an offer. In most cases, the seller will state an asking price. There is no reason that you must accept this price. The seller expects some negotiation and has probably included a margin that may be bargained away (see Key 20). However, too low an offer may cut off negotiations before they start. There are several points you should consider when coming up with an offering bid.

First, it is important to know how much you can afford to pay (see Key 9). It does no good to offer more than you can pay, which is the sum of the down payment and the amount to be financed. Part of the price you pay can come from a mortgage loan in the case of a condo (or a share loan for a co-op). There will be costs associated with the loan, so the actual cost to you will be higher. If you are short on cash, you may ask the seller to pay some of the discount points on the loan in return for a higher price. You may consider asking the seller to accept a second mortgage for part of the equity if there is a problem raising enough money for a down payment. On the other hand, you may have plenty of cash—especially if you sold your previous home for a profit—but are constrained by the size of the loan for which you can qualify.

Second, you should be aware of your alternatives. You probably are familiar with comparable units on the market if you have looked at many homes before settling on this one. How does the asking price of this unit compare to the others? More important, could you be satisfied with another unit if you can't make a deal on this one? If you can walk away from the negotiations with little reluctance, you are in a strong negotiating position and can afford to make a low offer. If you must have this unit, you will have to make more concessions.

Third, market conditions affect negotiation. In some markets, sellers must choose from many offers and may hold out for their asking price; there have even been cases where units have sold above the asking price. In other cases, sellers are fortunate to find any buyers at all and must make big price reductions. Indications of a buyer's market (where you have an advantage) are a large number of listings in the papers, homes that stay on the market for a long time, and ads that claim the price has been reduced. If you have had a problem with advertised homes selling before you had a chance to see them, that signals a seller's market. Obviously, you have more bargaining power in a buyer's market.

If the unit must be modified after you buy it, you should factor those costs into your offer. Even if you do not plan to make alterations, deduct from your offer if the property is not in top condition.

Finally, consider how strong an offer you are making. If your offer has important contingencies attached, you are in a weaker negotiating position. For example, if you must have VA financing and there is some question of your qualifying for the loan, the offer is not a strong one. If you must sell your current home in a slow market, the offer is very weak. If there is some reason to expect trouble getting the co-op board to approve your purchase, your offer is weakened. In these cases, you will not be able to negotiate a good price unless the market is very favorable toward buyers.

The key to making a good offer is to understand how the market works. Don't assume the seller's price is firm. Have an idea of a fair price for the unit and start out a bit lower. Know the strength of your bargaining position and what concessions you may reasonably obtain.

20

NEGOTIATION

Buying a home is not like buying merchandise in a retail store. In most cases, offering prices are not firmly set and some negotiation is expected before a sale is made. If you do not wish to get involved in haggling over price, you can pay the seller's price but you will probably be paying too much for the property. By no means should you rule out a property because the offering price is slightly higher than you can afford. If you like the home, at least find out if the seller is willing to deal. You don't have to offer a ridiculously low bid, but one more in line with what you think the home is worth.

Some buyers feel negotiation is unbecoming and are uncomfortable trying to obtain a lower price. Others relish the chance to drive a hard bargain. Most of us view negotiation as a means of getting a fair price. Don't let your fear of aggressiveness interfere with your true objective. After all, your purpose is to buy a home at a good price.

Good negotiation requires two types of understanding.

1. You should be well enough acquainted with the market to judge what the property is worth. Be aware of your alternatives. You should have an idea of the highest price at which the home is preferable to other acceptable homes on the market. If there are no acceptable alternatives, consider the option of not buying at all. You may stay where you are or, if transferring from out of town, find a rental home until new alternatives present themselves.

2. You should understand the negotiating process. A

sales contract is reached when there is an offer from one party and acceptance from the other party. In practical terms, this means that the contract is valid when both buyer and seller sign. Up to that point, you may break off the process by simply rejecting the offer. On the other hand, once you accept the seller's offer by signing the contract, you cannot alter the terms of the agreement.

Usually, a contract is arrived at through a series of offers and counteroffers. This is initiated by the buyer making an offer. The seller may counter by reducing his or her original price to something above the buyer's offer. These counteroffers may go back and forth until both parties agree. Price is not the only thing subject to negotiation. Who pays closing costs, what furnishings are included, repair work, and even the closing date may be negotiated (see Key 21).

The broker. A broker is usually involved in the negotiation process. Many people feel more comfortable dealing through a broker than dealing face to face with the other party. A broker can simplify the process considerably. You should be aware that the broker is working for the seller. The broker earns a commission only if the sale is successful, so he or she is willing to work closely with you to complete the negotiation. However, you should not rely on the broker for negotiating advice or ask about the seller's situation. An ethical broker cannot provide that type of information.

21

NEGOTIATION POINTS

When negotiating the purchase of a home, it is helpful to understand the various points of give-and-take that make up the transaction. It may be that some things are more important to you or the seller than the price of the unit. An effective negotiating strategy can be to give in to the seller's desired price while extracting concessions on other items. At the same time, realize that the more stipulations you add to the contract, the less likely you will be able to reduce the seller's price.

Among the more important points subject to negotiation are the following.

Price. This includes the dollar amount and how it is to be paid. In most cases, the entire amount is due in cash at closing. However, you may want to make a partial payment at closing and pay the rest at a later date, particularly if you are having trouble arranging for a down payment.

Closing costs. In some markets it is common to ask the seller to pay some or all discount points. Payment of additional points may allow you to get a loan with a lower rate of interest. Having the seller pay your closing costs conserves cash needed for the down payment. On the other hand, you may offer to pay closing costs commonly paid by the seller in exchange for a lower overall price. These expenses include title policy premiums and brokerage commissions. This tactic would be especially effective when the value of the property has declined and the seller is strapped for cash.

Financing. The seller may be willing to take a note for

all or a portion of the price. Frequently, when you are assuming the seller's existing loan, the seller will provide additional financing to make up the difference between the loan balance and the price. This opens up an entire new area for negotiation: the interest rate, term, timing of payments, and other items involving the loan. To the extent that these terms are better than what you can get from an outside lender, you are gaining advantages from the seller's financing that reduce the overall cost of the home.

Timing. The seller almost always wants the closing to be as soon as possible, unless the unit is currently occupied. You may have reasons to put off the closing— to raise a down payment, to sell other property, or to coincide with an intercity move. On the other hand, the seller may want to delay closing or your occupation of the property. The right to set a closing date may be a valuable point of negotiation if timing is critical. In addition, occupation before or after closing could be negotiated with rent paid for the intervening period.

Contingencies. Almost all sales are contingent on financing. However, if you are paying cash, or have financing already lined up, you are in a stronger position to bargain. Contingencies such as ability to sell another property may severely weaken your position. In strong markets, sellers may be unwilling to entertain such contracts. However, these are important escape clauses and you should insist on them if you need them. Consider that if you waive a contingency you are accepting the risk that you may forfeit your earnest money.

Property condition. In most cases the seller makes no warranties about the property's condition. However, you may require the property to be in working order as a condition of sale. This usually means you have the right to have a property condition inspection and can require the seller to make necessary repairs. If you are willing to take the property "as is," you should receive a price concession, especially when the property is in a distressed situation.

22

SALES CONTRACTS

In most northeastern states a *binder* is used to make an initial offer on a condo or co-op. When accepted, the owner agrees to take the property off the market and have an attorney prepare, in the next few days, a contract for the sale of the property (see the next Key for more information on binders).

In other areas, a *sales contract* formalizes the negotiation process between you and the seller. This form may be called a *contract of sale*, *agreement of sale*, or *earnest money contract* in different parts of the United States.

To make a binding offer, you must use a written contract; otherwise, the seller can't respond in any meaningful way. If you are working through a broker or agents, they will have preprinted standard contract forms. In some states the exact wording of the form is mandated by the state agency that regulates professional real estate licenses, called the real estate commission. Alternatively, you may have an attorney draft a contract for your purpose. However, the standard forms cover the most common items needed for the sale of a condo or co-op.

You should realize that once you submit an offer in the form of a sales contract, the seller may accept your offer by signing the contract. The contract then becomes binding on both you and the seller. If the seller counters, it will most likely be in the form of modifications to the contract you submitted. That contract does not become binding until you initial any changes. Negotiations will become more difficult if you begin to add new items to the contract. Therefore, you should be careful when making your first offer to include all items you want in the contract.

If you have never seen a sales contract, this discussion may be a little confusing. While the contract states the price you are willing to pay for the home, it also covers all conditions attached to the sale. Remember that the price is only one point in the negotiation of a sale. Agreement must be reached on how the price is met, timing of the sale, what is included in the sale, who pays sales costs, and under what conditions either party can back out of the sale.

All contracts identify the seller and buyer, the property involved, and the offered price. References to the property should include a legal description and identify what is to be included (any furnishings? mineral rights?). Price should be elaborated by stating the amount of cash down payment, money to be provided through a mortgage loan, and any money paid immediately as a deposit (earnest money).

The reason financing provisions are important is that most contracts include a contingency provision in case you are turned down for the loan. If you can't get the loan, this clause allows you to recover your earnest money. At the same time, it frees the seller to offer the home to another buyer. Generally, there are separate forms for conventional, FHA, and VA financing. The seller needs to know the type of financing, since some loans require the seller to pay discount points. This fact may affect negotiation.

Other contingencies may be placed in the contract for the protection of the buyer.

1. You may want to condition the sale on the property successfully passing inspections for physical condition and absence of wood-destroying insects. These provisions give you the right to have the property inspected (at your expense). If anything is found wrong, the seller has the option of repairing the problem or, if too costly, releasing you from the contract.

2. You may also require the right to void the sale if the property is found to be in a flood hazard area.
3. If you own a home currently, you may make the sale contingent on selling your home. The seller may ask for the right to accept back-up contracts from other potential buyers. If for some reason you fail to go through with the sale, the seller can offer the property to the holder of a back-up contract.

The contract sets a date for the closing and identifies who is responsible for the various expenses of sale. The latter provision is important if these expenses are not handled in the customary way. For example, if you want the seller to pay for discount points or if you are offering to pay the broker's commission, it should be stated in the contract.

If you do not understand a provision in the contract at any point in the negotiation, ask your broker or attorney to explain it. Once signed, the contract will dictate how the sale is conducted and will determine how much you pay and what you get for your money.

23

BINDERS AND ATTORNEY REVIEW PERIOD

In many states a purchase contract is called a *binder*. It does not have the force of law until after the expiration of an *attorney review period*, which is supposed to last three to five business days, depending on the state. At the end of this period, when the contract is acceptable to both parties, the buyer adds significantly to the deposit money.

While the avowed purpose of having an attorney review period may be to reduce a buyer's anxiety, the effect is often exactly the opposite. An attorney representing either the buyer or the seller may object to one or more provisions in the contract and may draft a contract addendum to substitute for the objectionable or unacceptable provisions. Then, ideally, working through the buyers, sellers, or their agents, the attorneys discuss their objections and make an effort to resolve the problems.

If your state is one with an attorney review period, you may be under time pressure to find an attorney who can help in the process. Don't expect either your attorney or the seller's to begin the review process on the day he or she receives the contract; the attorney has other things going on in his or her life or business. Don't be surprised if one of the attorneys waits until the last day of the review period to look at the contract—when the other attorney is busy in court with a different client and can't be reached.

The buyer's and seller's anxiety level will likely become elevated as the review period approaches expiration without a response from the other's attorney. Worse, one (or both) of the attorneys may be a bull in a china shop, overstepping the bounds of his or her assignment and zealously guarding his or her client's interests to the point of contract failure. The same may be true of the real estate agent, who provides answers to important questions as though he or she were a principal. Lawyers, it seems, view the home-buying process as one in which buyers and sellers are naturally antagonistic. In truth, they need each other.

During this attorney review period another buyer may come along who proposes to offer more money. The seller may then attempt to begin a bidding war whereby you are forced to pay a higher price or drop out. Often it is reality, but it could be a bluff. Potential buyers often say they're really interested until they're asked to put up money. Then they get cold feet. You'll have to decide whether to play the seller's favorite game or to back off. Much depends on your personal situation and market conditions.

24

ENVIRONMENTAL FACTORS

When buying a condo or co-op, be sure that the contract includes a provision for a physical inspection, including a search for contaminants. If a contaminant is found, the seller can probably choose either to remediate it, if the cost is within a certain specified amount, or to walk away from the deal. In new or converted properties, the developer/converter may be required to provide disclosure of these items.

As a buyer, you also want to include the right to walk away if certain contaminants are found, especially if you are concerned with the potential stigma effect. A *stigma* is a negative condition associated with contaminated property that has been remediated. The unpleasant associations remain even though the problem has been cured. For example, no matter how carefully it has been cleaned and refurbished, a dwelling that was the scene of a murder or other horrendous crime may remain stigmatized for a long time.

Common contaminants include asbestos, lead-based paint, underground storage tanks, and radon.

Asbestos. Asbestos is found in many dwellings, especially those built before the mid-1970s. It is often found in floor and ceiling tile, roofing materials, or siding, or as pipe wrap or coating for heating equipment.

Asbestos is not considered a health hazard unless it is in a *friable* state. This means it is crumbling, a state in which asbestos particles or fibers may become airborne. If fibers get into residents' lungs, they may cause cancer or another lung-related illness such as asbestosis.

The cheapest method of remediating asbestos is encapsulation. This involves spraying the asbestos with a special type of paint, thus containing it. While encapsulation (or wrap) may bring some peace of mind, it doesn't remove the problem—the special paint could someday be scratched and torn, exposing asbestos. Thus, the best policy is probably to hire a professional, licensed company to remove the asbestos. In most cases, a reasonable seller will agree to take care of the problem by arranging for repair or agreeing to pay the cost, up to a limit in the contract, of repairs arranged by the broker or buyer.

If the proposed purchase is loaded with asbestos, including floor or ceiling tile or roofing material, you might consult an expert about costs and choices. Keep in mind that laws tend to become more stringent and consumer tastes more demanding, so your acquisition, if not remediated, may become very difficult to resell.

Lead-based paint. Lead was commonly used in paints until 1978. If you're buying a dwelling that was built before 1978, it could contain lead-based paint. Sellers of dwellings built before 1978 must disclose the presence of such paint or indicate that they don't know whether it is present.

The potential hazard of lead-based paint is that children may eat the peelings. The only real solution for buyers of such units, short of stripping and sanding down all paint and starting from scratch, is, of course, to instruct children never to eat any paint that has peeled from walls or ceilings. This may or may not be effective depending on the age and obedience level of the children.

Radon. Radon is a natural substance that may appear in the ground, air, or water. An inspector will leave a test kit exposed to air inside the house for a few days and send a sample of water to a lab. Radon has been associated with lung cancer among workers in uranium mines. Mine worker results have been extended to dwellings, even though no scientific study has shown an association of illness with radon in homes.

If a high level of radon is detected in the air within a unit, its probable source is the ground around it under the slab or basement. Often a pipe may be inserted in the basement, through closets above, for release of radon-tainted air to the outside. This may remediate the problem. Check with your local health department for suggestions when a high level of radon appears in water or air and cannot be relieved by the simple method.

Underground storage tanks. Underground storage tanks have often been used for storing heating oil. If a tank is present in the premises you are considering, ask the seller to remove it. Generally, the local fire department is called to review the removal and to supervise the taking of soil samples. If soil contamination is found, further investigation may be required to determine the extent of migration, the proximity of underground water supply sources, and the cost of remediation.

EMF. At one time it was thought that proximity to high-voltage overhead electromagnetic field (EMF) wires was hazardous. This theory has been debunked. Still, you might not want to be near these eyesores.

25

MORTGAGE TYPES

Today it is not enough for a home buyer to know what a mortgage loan is. There are various types of loans available for financing the purchase of a home. You should have some understanding of the important differences among the loans if you want to get the loan that is best for you. The type of financing you choose can make a big difference in your ability to afford the home and the ultimate costs you will bear.

Insurance programs. Most lenders are willing to lend up to 80 percent of the home's value on a mortgage. However, many home buyers are unable or unwilling to contribute at least 20 percent of the cost of the home in cash. Therefore, the federal government, through the Federal Housing Administration (FHA), provides an insurance program that encourages lenders to make loans at higher loan-to-value ratios. If you get an FHA loan, your down payment may be as low as 3 percent of value. The lender makes the loan, but the FHA insures against the possibility that you will fail to make timely payments. This insurance is not free. You pay an up-front premium equal to 2.25 percent of the loan amount, which may be financed as part of the loan; this can be reduced to 1.75 percent for first-time home buyers who attend a special home-ownership seminar. In addition, there is a monthly premium for loans covering more than 90 percent of value.

Loans insured by the FHA have absolute maximum amounts that vary by location. Check with the local office of the FHA or HUD to find the limit for your area. There are private mortgage insurance (PMI) companies that provide similar coverage on loans of larger amounts. Private mortgage insurance premiums can be paid in a lump sum at closing or in annual or monthly payments. The costs depend on the loan-to-value ratio on the loan, how much coverage the lender requires, and whether the loan is fixed or variable. When shopping for a loan, ask for an estimate of how much the insurance premium will be.

VA loans. The Veterans Administration offers a guarantee program for eligible military veterans. If you are eligible, you can get a VA loan from a private lender with no down payment at all. This program is free to those who qualify. Any loan that is not insured by the FHA or guaranteed by the VA is called a "conventional" loan, even if covered by a PMI policy.

ARMs. Another important distinction in the loan market is the way interest is charged. Traditionally, mortgage loans have been made at a fixed rate of interest that never varied as long as you had the loan. Recently, loans have been introduced in which the interest rate may vary according to interest rates in the market.

These Adjustable-Rate Mortgages (ARMs) usually are originated at an interest rate below that of fixed-rate loans. However, you may be exposed to rising rates in the future that could make the loan more costly. When the interest rate rises (or falls), your monthly payments will increase (or decrease). To limit the risk of the rate rising too high, most ARMs have caps, which determine how high the rate may be raised in any one year, and a ceiling on the maximum rate the loan can bear. They may also have floors.

Buy-down loans. Another type of loan that may be used when interest rates are high is the "buy-down" loan. By paying additional points, the borrower (or the seller) can have the interest rate reduced. This may be critical to allow the buyer to pass underwriting standards for the loan (see Key 9, Affordability and Loan Qualifying). Often, the buy-down works to reduce the interest rate only for the first several years of the loan. The hope is that interest rates will fall in the meantime and you can refinance the loan.

Existing loans. Sometimes you can finance the purchase without getting a new loan. The seller may have an existing loan that you can assume. Most FHA and VA loans can be assumed by the buyer with no change in the interest rate. If the loan is conventional, the lender may refuse to allow the loan to be assumed or may raise the interest rate. In addition, the old loan may have a balance that is too far below the selling price. If you assume the loan, you will have to make up the difference in cash or with a second mortgage loan.

26

FINANCING A
CO-OP PURCHASE

Cooperative financing is more complicated than other
types of housing loans. This is because you are buying
shares of stock in a corporation that owns the building,
rather than the real estate itself. If you were buying real
estate, you could get a mortgage loan to cover most of
the cost of the property. The portion of the home's value
not covered by the mortgage is called *equity*. If you were
to sell the property with the buyer assuming the mortgage loan, the buyer would pay you an amount equal to
the equity. In general, most buyers would make this payment from their cash savings, although they could take
out a second mortgage for part of it.

When you buy co-op shares, it is similar to buying a
home with an assumption. The corporation probably has
a mortgage loan on the property, so the amount of
"equity" is reduced and this should be reflected in the
price of the shares. If this equity is not large, you may be
able to buy the shares without the assistance of financing. However, there may be no mortgage loan on the
property, or the amount may have been paid down, or the
value of the building may have increased since the loan
was originated. In these cases, the price of the shares
may be so high that financing is required.

Two factors may make co-op loans more expensive
than home mortgage loans. First, you cannot give the
lender a mortgage on the real estate, or your unit, since
you don't own it. You can pledge your stock in the co-
op, but that is not considered as secure from a collateral
standpoint as the title to a home. Second, if the co-op is

mortgaged, the lender would have less security in case the corporation defaulted on the mortgage loan.

If you need financing for the purchase, check with the co-op board for good sources of co-op share loans. If cooperative housing is common in your area, local lenders may have special loans available. If not, you may have to take out an expensive, personal loan. There are special lending programs for co-op housing since the Federal National Mortgage Association (FNMA, or Fannie Mae), a private company affiliated with the government, began buying portfolios of such loans. The co-op must be approved before you can get one of these loans.

The FHA insures loans used to buy cooperative housing shares through its 203(n) program. Check local lenders for availability. Most of the features of this financing are the same as for the 203(b) program applied to single-family residences. That means, for instance, that a co-op could be purchased with as little as a 3 percent down payment.

However, it should be recognized that the same maximum loan size limits that apply to the single-family program also apply to this program.

27

FINANCING A
CONDO PURCHASE

Unlike co-ops, you can finance the purchase of a condo with a home mortgage loan. In general, you have access to all the types of loans and loan sources normally used for home buying. This includes FHA and VA loans, as well as the various loan varieties such as ARMs (see Key 25 on Mortgage Types). Savings and loan associations, mutual savings banks, commercial banks, mortgage banking companies, and credit unions make condominium loans.

The procedure for applying for a condo loan is the same as for any mortgage loan. You need to take a copy of your sales contract and information on your income, source of down payment, and other assets and liabilities to the lender and make a formal loan application. The lender will process your application and provide a loan commitment if the loan is approved.

You should be aware that there have been times in some areas when loans for condos were not available. In severely depressed markets, lenders have been reluctant to finance condos because they considered them difficult to sell in the event the borrower defaulted. Even when lenders are willing to make loans, the rates they offer may be higher than for detached homes. It is a good practice to ask lenders about loan availability and rates before you sign a sales contract. Also find out if the condo project is FHA- and/or FNMA-approved as this may open up additional sources of financing, or restrict financing availability.

The FHA insures condo loans under its 234(c) program. This means that lenders can provide loans with as little as a 3 percent down payment when FHA insurance is applied. The development must be approved by the FHA, and insurance premiums must be paid along with the closing costs and monthly payment. Most of the rules applied to this program are the same as those applied to the FHA 203(b) program that purchasers of single-family homes often use.

Include in your contract to purchase the condo a financing requirement; if you cannot arrange the financing you seek, you will not be committed to buy, and you can get a refund of your deposit.

If mortgage loans are unavailable at affordable rates, you may be able to arrange a loan with the seller. When loans are not available, sellers know that they must provide financing to sell their units. If you know this to be the case before you conclude negotiations, you can include the financing terms in the negotiation process (see Key 21, Negotiation Points). There may also be the possibility of assuming the existing mortgage loan.

Prearranged financing. A condo that has been recently built or converted may have prearranged financing available. Often, builders and converters arrange financing for the entire project that can be applied for by individual buyers of the units. This financing may carry more favorable terms than those available from outside lenders.

These loans are offered as an inducement to sales and should be taken advantage of if you find the unit acceptable and competitively priced.

Purchase and rehabilitation financing. If the condo unit you are considering needs a lot of work, you might consider a loan that combines purchase and rehabilitation financing. Such funding can be had using a loan insured under the FHA's 203(k) program. Essentially, these loans provide sufficient money to buy the unit and fix it up with only a minimal cash investment from the borrower. While the program is designed for detached single-family homes, condo units are eligible. The borrower must also intend to live in the unit. Rehab work funded, though the loan is restricted to the interior space (legally, the exterior is the responsibility of the owners' association). The amount of the loan can exceed the current value of the unit but must not be for more than the total value of the unit after the work is done. Check your local FHA office for more details and specifics for your area.

28

THE CLOSING

The closing is the official end of all preliminaries and the beginning of your ownership period in your new home. In simple terms, the closing is a meeting where you provide the purchase price and the seller gives you a deed to the property. However, closings are rarely that simple. In reality, there are many things that must be settled and paid for at the closing.

Most of the people involved in the transaction will be present or have a representative at the closing. Foremost among this group are the lender, the broker(s), and the title company. In addition, both buyer and seller may have legal counsel present. The lender will forward the money you arranged to borrow and record the mortgage on the property. The brokers will collect their commissions for arranging the sale. The title company provides title insurance policies and may act as an escrow agent as well. The escrow agent collects all funds and disburses them to the appropriate accounts.

There are several fees and charges you will be expected to pay at closing. Fortunately, you can review a good faith estimate of these charges before you go to the closing. Federal law (the Real Estate Settlement Procedures Act) gives you the right to review the figures on the closing papers before closing and requires that specific forms be used. These forms provide an itemized list of the expenses you and the seller are required to pay. With the help of your attorney, you should review the forms and make sure they conform to your sales contract.

The following are items commonly charged to the buyer. Some of these may become the responsibility of the seller if specifically negotiated in the contract.

- *Down payment.* This is the difference between the loan amount(s) and the sales price.

- *Loan expenses.* These include the origination fees, discount points, assumption fee, if the loan is assumed, and mortgage insurance premium, if an insured loan is used.

- *Prorated insurance premium.* If the existing insurance policy is not replaced with a new policy, you must pay a portion of the premium for the remainder of the current term. If you are getting a new policy, you will need to provide the premium for the next year. In addition, the lender will require you to fund the escrow account that pays insurance and taxes in future years.

- *Government fees.* There are a number of fees charged for recording documents.

- *Prepaid interest.* The lender requires interest to be paid for the time between the closing day and the beginning of the loan term, usually the beginning of the next month.

- *Attorney fees.* If you use an attorney, the fee is collected at closing.

- *Survey and inspections.* The lender usually requires a new boundary survey to be conducted, for which you pay. Most contracts require a termite inspection. If you had a physical inspection of the property, the fee is often collected at closing.

The seller also has a list of expenses due at closing. These usually include

- Broker's commission.

- Prorated property taxes representing the time from the beginning of the tax year to the closing day.

- Attorney's fee.

- Title insurance premium.

- Transfer taxes.

- Any repairs that resulted from inspections of the property.

Be prepared to present a certified or cashier's check to cover your portion of closing expenses. Handled properly, the closing can be a smooth and agreeable beginning of life in your new home.

29

THE SPECIAL CASE OF CONVERSIONS

Because condominiums and cooperatives are physically similar to rental apartments, it is relatively easy to convert from one to the other. The process is more of a legal one than a development project, although some physical remodeling is done to enhance salability of the units. A landlord may convert for one of many reasons: the property no longer makes sense as a rental (in some areas, rent control laws may be hurting the property's investment performance), the property may be sold at a much higher price if converted, or there is growing demand for owner-occupied housing in the market.

If the conversion process is handled well, the property should be as attractive as any other condo or co-op. However, there are many potential problems in the transition from rental to owner-occupied. If you are buying into such a situation, or are a current tenant facing the decision to buy your apartment, you will want to take steps to avoid such problems.

The basic fact of conversion is that, once you have purchased a unit, all the problems of the property are your responsibility rather than the landlord's. Therefore, you will want to know what potential problems exist so that you can be prepared to deal with them. You should have an expert locate needed repairs and conditions that will require attention in the near future. Even if you currently live in the building, there may be many faults that you are unaware of. In many cases, the converter will establish a reserve fund to take care of these problems. Make sure the fund is adequate for the job.

Management. Management of converted buildings is often a problem. If the management company stays on after the conversion, the homeowners' association or co-op board should have some way of replacing the manager if he or she is not working in the best interests of the owner-tenants. If the manager has a long-term contract (more than three years), it may be broken by a vote of two-thirds of the board under the provisions of the federal Condominium and Cooperative Abuse Relief Act.

Be aware that a new board may require time to learn its duties and to assert its authority. This is a time when the landlord or converter may push through actions that favor his or her interests over the tenants.

Selling to existing tenants. Converters are usually interested in selling units to existing tenants. The tenants represent a ready-made market and selling avoids the problems of moving tenants out to make way for the new owners. Existing tenants may be offered special "insider" prices for their units, often 25 percent below the initial offering price. There may even be financing provided or arranged by the converter. If you are interested in buying, these inducements can be valuable; check to see whether the discounts and financing arrangements are indeed real by comparing them to comparable units and outside financing.

Remaining a rental tenant. If you want to stay, but can't afford to buy or are unwilling to buy, you may have some rights to remain a rental tenant under state or local law. For example, in New York this depends on whether the conversion was approved as a noneviction plan. The elderly and handicapped may have additional rights. You or the existing tenants as a group may need to consult an attorney to determine what you can do. If you have to move, the converter may offer some form of relocation assistance. In most instances, the converter will want to make your transition as easy as possible to speed along the marketing effort.

When buying into a converted building, you may

want to find out how many units remain as rental units. The conversion may not have been a complete success. If the majority are rented, the project will probably not function well as a condo or co-op. Even if most are owned by tenants, the owner of the rental units may hold power over the board, since he or she controls the votes of the rental units. This landlord may not share the interests of the other owners and conflicts are highly likely. A buyer should approach such situations with caution.

Sponsor default. Another issue is the possibility of sponsor default. If the former landlord or a "converter" owns a large number of units and has insufficient cash flow to pay the expenses connected with such ownership, he or she may default on his or her obligations to pay maintenance. In such cases the board may be hard-pressed to pay its bills, placing the entire cooperative in jeopardy. (See Keys 28 and 49.)

As mentioned in Key 27, you can use FHA-insured mortgages to buy a condo unit. However, there are some special restrictions when the unit is a conversion. In most cases, the FHA will not insure a loan for a conversion until the process is at least a year old. On the other hand, if you are a tenant in a building that is being converted, or if the conversion is being done by a tenants' organization, the FHA will waive the one-year restriction. This means that, if you are looking at a unit in a building being converted, you will probably not be able to use FHA financing.

30

CONDOMINIUM DOCUMENTS

To make an informed choice when buying a condo unit, you will need to inspect the major legal documents defining the condo. It is a good idea to use an experienced real estate attorney to help you interpret the language of these documents. You should also have an idea of what these documents are.

The declaration. The document that legally sets the property up as a condominium is the *declaration*. Your interest in the declaration is finding out just what your individual interests in the property will be. You should be able to determine the extent of your individual interest (do you own the exterior walls or your enclosed patio, for example) and what is considered common property. In addition, you will want to know what proportion of the total complex is allocated to your interest. This proportion determines your share of voting rights and association expenses.

The bylaws. Closely related to the declaration is the *bylaws*. There are two parts of this document with which you will want to be familiar. The first is the description of how the association is governed and the procedures for electing officers and getting approvals. This is like a constitution for the association and it defines your political rights in condominium affairs. Even if you are unconcerned about how the association is run, you will want to examine closely the second part of the bylaws. This part sets out the restrictions that each owner agrees to abide by. Other Keys have discussed restrictions that may cause you problems. Look through the bylaws before you commit to buying the unit.

Budget and financial statements. You may want to examine the association's budget and financial statements prior to purchase. These documents should be made available to you. If not, the seller or association may be trying to hide something. If the condo is relatively new, you might expect significant changes in expenses over the next few years. If the complex has been running for some time, the old budgets may be a good indication of the future.

Unit deed. At the closing, you will receive a *unit deed* to the property. The deed establishes your ownership. The document will probably repeat much of the information in the declaration. The language in your deed should be consistent with all other documents pertaining to the condominium.

31

CO-OP
DOCUMENTS

When you buy into cooperative housing, you play
two roles. First, you are a shareholder in the corporation
that owns and operates the building. Second, you are a
tenant in that building, unless you are subleasing your
unit. Each role carries certain rights and responsibilities,
which are defined in special legal documents. When
shopping for a co-op unit, do not assume that all cooperatives are set up the same way. You will need to critically examine the legal documents to see what kind of
restrictions will apply.

Co-op bylaws. The co-op *bylaws* are similar in function to the condominium bylaws. They describe how the
co-op is run and the rules that apply to share owners.
Here you will learn the makeup of the board, how members are elected, and what their duties are. There may be
important restrictions on what you can do with your
apartment, such as subleasing, and how you can sell
your interests, such as the right of first refusal for the
board. It is essential that you be familiar with these
restrictions before you commit to buying.

Stock certificates. When you buy into a co-op, you
will be issued *stock certificates* in the corporation. These
serve a purpose similar to the deed you would receive if
you had bought a condo. They are the proof of your
ownership and indicate how much of a share of the corporation you control. In practice, you may never use the
actual certificates since they may be held as security for
the loan you used to buy your shares.

Proprietary lease. As a resident in the building, the

most important document to you is the *proprietary lease*, which establishes your right to occupy a certain apartment in the building. Its purpose and structure are much like any apartment lease you have signed. The big difference is that the term of the lease is not a specified period but is contingent on your ownership of the shares. There will be language in the lease that sets out the conditions under which you may lose your right to occupy the unit. There are also provisions for your maintenance fee or rent payments and other restrictions placed on how you can use your unit and the common areas. This lease should also be examined carefully prior to purchase. Key 32 provides an overview of important proprietary lease provisions.

Budget and financial statements. You may want to look at the corporation's budget and financial statements as well. These will give you an idea of what expenses you can expect and how well prepared the co-op is for unexpected expenses.

32

THE CO-OP PROPRIETARY LEASE

When you buy shares in a co-op, you will also sign a document called a *proprietary lease*. This gives you the right to occupy a specific unit in the building. This lease is similar to a standard apartment lease used for rental properties. However, there are some important differences.

Term. A co-op lease states no definite term for your occupancy. You are entitled to occupy the unit for as long as you own shares in the co-op and do not violate provisions of the lease. These provisions are covered in the lease in detail. Generally, they will include your obligation to pay maintenance fees and other required expenses of ownership, to conduct yourself within the restraints specified in the lease, and to refrain from making unauthorized alterations to the unit. The lease will describe the conditions under which you may be evicted from the unit. If you are evicted, the co-op board may be able to sell your shares and lease your unit to the new owner. Provisions for selling your shares and what happens to the money are included in the lease.

Rent. The lease acknowledges the number of shares you own and specifies which unit you occupy. There is no stated rent amount. However, the lease mentions your obligation to pay regular maintenance fees and other charges as determined by the board.

Subordination. The lease may include a clause that allows you to borrow against your shares in the co-op.

This clause gives the lender first claim to the value of the shares over other claimants, such as the holder of the mortgage on the building or the board itself.

Other portions of the lease are much like rental leases, such as a list of restrictions on what you can do in and with the unit and provisions for subleasing or assigning the unit. This states the conditions under which you can substitute a tenant and whether the board must approve the new tenant. There may also be some provision for the board to share part of the rent.

The proprietary lease is an important document and should be reviewed prior to buying shares in the co-op. Pay particular attention to the "house rules" listed in the lease, as these may limit your enjoyment of your new home.

33

CO-OP SHAREHOLDERS' RIGHTS AND RESPONSIBILITIES

Home ownership in general carries with it certain rights and responsibilities. You have the right to enjoy your property within the limits imposed by the rights of other property owners. You have the right to sell your home when the need or desire arises. In conjunction with these rights, you have the responsibility to keep the property in decent condition and fulfill any financial obligations entailed in ownership, such as paying your mortgage and property taxes.

The same rights and responsibilities apply to co-op housing. However, they may be constrained to account for the fact that you are sharing the facility with other residents. There is no denying that your freedom to enjoy your property is reduced. On the other hand, you may benefit from the fact that your neighbors are similarly constrained. The limits placed on individual co-op residents are intended to make living together more manageable. If you find such an arrangement distasteful, you are probably not well suited to co-op living.

The co-op board. The co-op board plays a crucial role in making the complex livable. You will find that the board has a lot to say about how you exercise your ownership rights. You must get its approval to become an owner and thus move into the building. Also, it must approve whomever you sell your unit to. It will set maintenance fees and collect them. The board also has the right to take action to end your right to occupy the unit if you fail to comply with the obligations of a resident or owner.

The board is not an arbitrary group of residents with dictatorial powers. It is selected by the owners and charged with the job of enforcing the bylaws of the co-op. You have the right to examine these bylaws prior to purchase. Once you are an owner, you have a vote in selecting board members. You also have a voice at owners' meetings and can help decide issues or bring about changes in the rules. This may seem like a lot of politics but that is an unavoidable fact of co-op living. If your interests and lifestyle are similar to the majority of residents, you will often be on the winning side. If not, life in the co-op may prove frustrating. This is one reason that screening prospective owners is important.

You may find that the board is too lax in performing its duties. Important violations of the bylaws may go without response, fees may fail to be collected, repair work may not get done, or favoritism may occur in decisions. In most cases, residents have the right to demand performance from the board and may even bring suit to force a recalcitrant board to take action. However, remember that the board must apply the rules to real-life situations and some room must be allowed for reasonableness.

To protect your rights as a co-op owner, it is important to understand

- How the board is selected.
- How expenses are distributed and income is collected.
- How to petition the board for action or approval.
- Procedures for the sale of your shares.
- What the specific house rules allow and prohibit.

34

CO-OP
TENANCY

Your right to occupy an apartment in a co-op building is established by the proprietary lease. The term of the lease is indefinite; however, it can be terminated by the board under certain conditions. In other words, even though you are a homeowner, you may lose your right to your home if you fail to comply with provisions of the proprietary lease.

The conditions under which your lease may be terminated are detailed in the proprietary lease. Some commonly stated situations are as follows:

- If for any reason, you no longer own the shares in the co-op.
- When you declare bankruptcy. In this case, the shares may become subject to rulings of the bankruptcy court.
- If you violate provisions of the lease, such as subletting or altering the unit without approval, objectionable behavior by you or other occupants, and failure to comply with some covenant in the lease. The most important provision, however, is the requirement to pay periodic maintenance fees and assessments.
- Situations where the co-op is dissolved, such as destruction or condemnation of the building or cancellation of a large majority of leases by the tenants.

Naturally, if you sell your shares, a new lease will be prepared for the new owner. However, if your lease is cancelled because you did not comply with the proprietary lease, you can be evicted. There will be provisions for what happens to the unit and your shares in the co-op. These are described in the lease. In general, the board will cancel your shares and issue new shares that can be sold by the board. The new owner of the shares gets a new lease. Until that time, your obligation to pay fees continues. The money from the sale of the new shares goes to satisfying any unpaid fees you may have left and any expenses incurred by the board in taking action. If anything is left, you may have the right to it. The action is very much like a foreclosure sale applied to a mortgage.

Evicting tenants is not something a co-op board enjoys. You should find that, if a problem arises, the board is willing to work with you to resolve it without the need for drastic action. However, an effective board must address situations that threaten the financial soundness and social atmosphere of the co-op. Otherwise, a small group of irresponsible tenants could spoil the ability of all the residents in the building to enjoy their homes.

35

FEES, RENT, AND MAINTENANCE

All condos and co-ops require payment of periodic fees by each resident. In condos, these are called *association fees*. In co-ops, they are usually called *maintenance*. In either case they have the same purpose: to provide money to the board or homeowners' association for meeting the expenses of running the property.

In condos, most of the budget is devoted to the common areas. The association must maintain the lawns, parking lots, lobbies, and any recreational facilities. There may also be provisions for repair and maintenance of the building's interior and exterior. Expenses may include liability insurance on the premises.

Co-op expenses cover common area maintenance as well as some items that are the responsibility of individual co-op owners. These may include property taxes and payments on a mortgage loan for the building. In general, co-op maintenance fees will be higher than those for a comparable condo. However, the co-op owner has fewer individual expenses. This is important to keep in mind when comparing purchase of a co-op with a condo.

The budget. Each year the board or association prepares a budget of expected expenses. Owners are assessed a pro rata share of the total expense. The division may be made equally per unit, per share, or according to the space occupied or the relative value of the units. You may expect that the fee will be raised each year as expenses increase. However, there should be no provision for some owners to be locked in to a fee so that the increase falls on other owners.

Unscheduled needs. In addition to the budgeted expenses, there will be unscheduled needs that inevitably occur. The board or association should have some means for addressing these problems. Some groups like to keep regular fees at a minimum and prefer to assess owners separately as the need arises. Low fees help to make the units more acceptable on the market. However, the need for a special assessment may hamper the ability of the board to respond to emergencies, such as repairing damage left by a storm. An assessment may also be a hardship on some owners operating on a strict budget. It is good practice for the board to maintain some type of reserve for such emergencies. Such a reserve may not avoid special assessments altogether, but should make them less frequent.

Improvement costs. Some complexes undertake improvements, generally in the form of expanding or adding recreational facilities. These plans can be a source of conflict among owners. The proponents of the improvements must battle with those who do not care for the facilities and do not want to pay for them. Other problems may occur if some owners desire high-quality maintenance while others want economy.

36

WHAT HAPPENS IF YOU DON'T PAY YOUR FEES?

As noted earlier, living in a condo or co-op is like being a resident of a small community. The condo fees or co-op maintenance are like the taxes you pay to the community. They go to provide services for the whole group. If you don't pay your share, the consequences can be as severe as if you failed to pay your taxes.

In a condo, delinquent fees could lead to the association filing a claim against your unit. After going to court, the association may obtain the right to force the sale of your unit and collect the unpaid fees and costs from the proceeds.

In a co-op, the board could evict you as a tenant and reissue the shares that you own (see Key 34). The exact procedure should be described in your proprietary lease.

Losing your home because of failure to pay fees seems drastic, but it is the only way the board or association has to enforce the fee requirement. It is a good idea to familiarize yourself with the procedures described in the bylaws or lease for enforcing the collection of the fee. You should also be sure that you can handle the fee within your budget before you decide to buy.

If an emergency occurs and you are temporarily unable to meet your obligation, you should inform the board or association officers. It is in the interest of the board or association to keep your unit and not have to bring legal action. They may be willing to help you work out a solution to the problem, such as temporarily reducing the fee or allowing you to skip the fees with the provision that you pay the arrears later with interest. The association will be in a better position to do something like this if they have a reserve built up than if they are operating on a thin budget margin. Nevertheless, your obligation to pay fees should never be taken lightly and you should not ignore appeals from the board for timely payment.

37

PROPERTY TAXES

All owners of real property must pay taxes to local government units. Generally these property taxes are assessed by the city, county, school district, and any other special district established to provide some public service. Property taxes are based on the value of your property. The local assessor prepares an appraisal of your property that, in conjunction with the tax rate, determines how much your tax will be. Often there is a partial exemption if the property is your principal residence (the homestead exemption).

Property taxes are applied to condos and co-ops just as they are to other types of property. With a condo, each owner is assessed a tax based on the value of the unit. Taxes applied to common areas should be included in this assessment, since the value of these areas is reflected in the value of your unit. If you have a mortgage loan on the unit, you will probably pay the tax through monthly contributions to an escrow account maintained by the lender. The actual payment is made by the lender or the company that services your loan. You are allowed to deduct from your federal taxable income any property taxes paid during the year for the purpose of calculating income taxes. Your lender should provide you with an indication of the amount of taxes paid.

The situation is different with co-ops. Property taxes for the whole building are paid by the board. A prorated share of these taxes is part of your monthly maintenance fee. However, you are still allowed to deduct your share of the taxes from your income taxes. The board should provide you a statement that reflects the amount of tax per share of the co-op you own. Special income tax laws allow a co-op owner to deduct the taxes that the co-op organization paid. This deduction is claimed in the same place as for a home or condo owner, Schedule A of Form 1040.

Failure to pay property taxes can lead to loss of your property. Local governments have the authority to force the sale of your property to satisfy delinquent taxes. Furthermore, should you go bankrupt, the local government's claim is superior to claims from other creditors. This is one reason that lenders maintain an escrow account to ensure that property taxes are paid. If you are paying your maintenance fee or escrow payments and you receive notice that taxes have not been paid, you should immediately take action to deal with the problem. It may be that your lender or the co-op board has not been diligent in paying the taxes, and you must clear up the problem.

38

INSURING YOUR HOME

All homeowners should have insurance to cover the possibility of property damage or destruction and the liability of potential injury to others while on their property. Typically, a homeowner's policy protects from three unfortunate possibilities: that your home will be damaged or destroyed in a fire or other accident, that your personal belongings will be destroyed or stolen, and that someone visiting your home will be injured and take legal action against you. As you can see, any of these events could be financially devastating if you do not have coverage.

Your co-op board or condo association probably will have insurance covering hazards and liability for the building and common areas. You pay a share of the premiums for this coverage either as part of your monthly fee or in a special assessment. However, in order to be adequately covered, you will need to provide additional insurance on your own unit.

If you live in a co-op, this additional policy will be similar to a renter's policy. It covers your personal belongings and liability within your unit. A tenant's policy should suffice, but if the company offers a special co-op owner's policy, you probably should get that.

Condo owners should get the type of policy especially designed for condominiums. These policies cover you where the condo association's policy leaves off. Because of the peculiarities of different condo arrangements, a tenant's policy would not be sufficient to give you good coverage.

You should also be aware that you may need special coverage beyond the standard homeowner's policy. These policies do not cover damage from floods. If your unit is in a flood-prone area, you may want to obtain special flood insurance. In addition, you may have personal items that are not fully covered, such as collectibles and expensive silver, art, furs, or jewelry. You may purchase additional coverage for these items.

Suppose your condominium association has no insurance. You may purchase a regular homeowner's policy to cover your unit. The weakness of this situation is the lack of uniformity from one unit to the next. If your neighbor carries insufficient insurance, he or she may not be able to rebuild after extensive damage. Since the structure of each unit is dependent on surrounding units, the whole building must be reconstructed for any unit to be sound. If your association does not have a policy, you should urge the board to look into the costs of obtaining adequate coverage. In many cases, the pro rata share of one uniform policy is lower than individual premiums for similar coverage.

39

REPAIRS AND MAINTENANCE

One of the advantages of condo or co-op ownership is freedom from the financial responsibility of repairs and the chore of property upkeep. Most of these problems are handled by the board or association. You pay for this through your monthly fee or special assessment but you may not escape totally from the need to make some repairs.

In most cases, you will be expected to take care of things within your unit. This includes interior painting and remodeling, routine housekeeping, replacing furnace filters, and keeping plumbing fixtures and kitchen appliances in working order. This is one of the big differences between owning an apartment and renting one from someone else. (If the condo or co-op has its own maintenance staff to take care of these items, you may be prevented from doing your own repairs. Check your lease for such provisions.)

There may be several areas where the division of personal and association responsibility is vague. Examples of such "gray areas" are

- *Exterior painting.* Since the exterior affects the appearance of the whole complex, the association will probably prevent individual owners from painting their own units. If yours needs painting, you will have to petition the association. The chances of the association undertaking the project will be smaller if your unit is the only one affected. You may be required to pay for the work. When the entire complex is painted, you may be able to determine the color, if that is the consensus of the owners.

- *Fencing.* In some complexes, privacy fencing is provided to help make each unit a little more distinctive. When it is time to replace these fences, the association should take over the job. If yours is the only one that needs fixing, however, you may be asked to pay for the work.
- *Plantings.* In some complexes, individual owners are allowed to maintain outdoor plants or may take on the responsibility of watering and caring for plants near their unit. Problems could occur if you use too much water (when units are not on individual meters) or dangerous pesticides.
- *Equipment.* Some equipment that serves your unit, such as a hot water heater, may also affect other units. For example, if a hot water heater is improperly installed, it could pose a danger to the entire building. In these cases, the association may discourage individual repairs and require the work to be done under the auspices of the association.

In addition to reviewing the policies of the board or association in these areas, you should ask for specifics that often are not spelled out in the bylaws and lease. Knowing what you are likely to get into is preferable to being surprised after you have taken some action.

40

PROPERTY IMPROVEMENTS, ALTERATIONS, AND REPAIRS

Part of the enjoyment of owning your home is customizing it to suit your tastes. This may range from repainting a room to adding a room or other major structural work. As you may suspect, your ability to alter your condo or co-op unit to your preference is more limited than if you owned a detached home. Once again, you will be affected by the give-and-take of collective living.

There are some advantages to this situation. If an improvement is desired by the majority of owners, you may have the benefit of it without having to bear the cost alone. This works well with such things as swimming pools and tennis courts. Also, you are somewhat protected from the ambitions of your neighbors. This may prevent your neighbor from installing a satellite dish outside your front door.

The disadvantages are obvious. You may be prevented from adding something to your property that you desire. This can be more than a mere inconvenience. For example, in some units, residents have been prevented from installing burglar bars in the windows because of objections to their appearance. Perhaps the individual wishing to make the alteration had been burglarized and was concerned about more than appearance. On the other hand, you may be required to help pay for improvements that you do not want or plan to use. Again, it is important to share interests and lifestyle preferences with your neighbors when you live in a condo or co-op.

You should not get the impression that alterations are impossible. Most condos and co-ops have provisions for individual tenant changes to the building. Generally, you will be required to submit a description of the change to the board for approval. Keep in mind the reasons why the board generally wants to control alterations. Its concern will be that your change does not alter the exterior appearance of the building in a way that would be objectionable to the other tenants, or that your work does not create an unsafe condition or nuisance for your neighbors. An example of an appearance change that might not be approved would be installing an outdoor television antenna on the roof or repainting the outside of the unit in some garish color. An unsafe condition might be created if you installed an electrical appliance that overloaded the circuits in the building and increased the chance of fire.

Suppose you fail to get approval, or neglect to inform the board, but go ahead with the change. Your co-op lease or condo bylaws should state what steps the board can take in such cases. The board may have the authority to require you to return the property to its former condition or to go in and do the work itself at your expense. Even if the board has a history of not enforcing the rules, you should respect its authority and proceed with caution.

It is a good idea to become familiar with the rules on improvements, alterations, and repairs and to discuss the matter with the board if you are planning any work. You will probably find that you can do a great deal with the board's approval and it will be reasonable to work with. Once a confrontation is created, however, that spirit of cooperation may vanish.

41

PROPERTY MANAGEMENT

While the board of the condo or co-op may make decisions, someone must carry out the work entailed to get things done. In small complexes, these tasks are often performed by the board or other owners. As the scale of the complex increases, the work necessary just for routine maintenance is too much for unpaid owners to do. It then becomes necessary to have a handyman or other paid employee to keep things going. It is also possible to hire firms to perform lawn maintenance, cleaning, pool maintenance, and other regular jobs. Larger complexes have a professional property manager to oversee the entire process.

Professional management firms usually specialize in this type of work or are a subsidiary of a real estate company. They are hired under a contract usually lasting one or more years. Fees for such services vary considerably, so it is necessary for the board to get competing bids from firms in the field. The duties assigned to the firm may vary, but can include

- *Handling maintenance and minor repairs.* The firm may have its own staff of maintenance employees, supervise a staff employed by the complex, or act as a contractor with independent service companies.
- *Getting major repair work done.* This includes getting bids from contractors, preparing a budget, awarding a contract, and supervising the work.
- *Collecting fees.* The firm may provide a billing

service and collect and deposit fees in the association or board account.

- *Consulting.* The firm may be helpful to the board in making decisions about repairs, improvements, or changing the way things are done.
- *Records.* The firm may be asked to prepare records of expenditures, budgets, tax forms, and reports to owners.

In addition, management for co-ops will likely take on more duties, such as paying regular bills for the association. Co-op boards usually have a more comprehensive list of responsibilities than condo boards.

Good management usually results in having an attractive and well-maintained complex. Likewise, bad management may stand out. If you are thinking of buying, pay close attention to how well things are maintained. You might talk to the management firm.

If the management of your complex is not satisfactory, you should lodge a complaint with the board. If enough people object, they should be able to terminate the contract soon and get a new firm. If nothing happens, even though most owners are dissatisfied, you may suspect that there is some special relationship between the board and the management firm. Sometimes, when the original developer or converter is still involved, contracts with management firms are not competitively bid. Check with your attorney for legal remedies available in your state for such situations.

42

RECREATIONAL FACILITIES

One of the advantages of living in a condo or co-op is having access to recreational facilities. Not everyone desires such amenities, but for those who do, a condo or co-op with the right facilities is a more reasonable alternative to buying a home and building your own private facilities. Those at your home are more convenient than using public parks and recreation areas.

The cost for this convenience includes rules that limit your use of the facilities, the additional fees needed to maintain them, and the potential for conflict among residents over issues relating to the facilities. The rules are necessary to make the facilities more useful to the majority of residents. For example, there may be periods when children are not allowed at the pool to give the adults a chance to swim in relative quiet. All facilities will need some maintenance, and some portion of your fee must go to provide for this. Conflicts may arise over the rules, enforcement of the rules, maintenance, or expansion and/or upgrade of the facilities.

Therefore, if you do not intend to use recreational facilities, you should find a home that does not have them; otherwise, you will be taking on costs without getting benefits that you enjoy. In addition, you may expect that the presence of facilities will tend to attract residents who do intend to use them.

The most popular facilities are pools and tennis courts. There may also be a general purpose recreational center with game rooms and areas that can be reserved for parties. Larger complexes may have health centers and organized social programs. Recreation facilities are one way that a complex can be custom-tailored for a specific market, such as young singles, families with small children, or senior citizens.

Here are some things to check:

- *Restrictions on use.* What hours are the facilities open? What conditions must be observed? Can you include children or pets? Do you need to reserve time of use? Are there user fees or admission costs? The restrictions may make the facilities less valuable to you than you first thought.
- *Safety.* Are the facilities safe to use? Is there supervision, such as a lifeguard on duty? Are the facilities too crowded when you want to use them?
- *Maintenance.* Are the facilities attractive and well maintained? Do they contribute to property values? Are maintenance duties entrusted to residents who perform them at their convenience, or is there a regular program?
- *Additions and expansions.* Are there plans for new facilities, remodeling, or expansion? How much will the improvements add to the monthly fee or special assessment? If a facility you desire is promised but not currently in place, expect that there is a good chance it will never be produced.

43

WORKING WITH THE OPERATING BOARD

It is a fact of life that if you live in a condo or co-op, you will eventually have dealings with the board. The board exercises an important role in keeping everything running properly and avoiding conflicts among residents. Taking the time to understand what the board does and how it does it is worthwhile.

No matter what the size of the complex and whether or not professional property management is used, the board is made up of homeowners who have been selected by the other homeowners in the complex. In general, a meeting of all homeowners will be held each year. In addition to other business conducted at this meeting, a new board is elected. The bylaws of the condo or co-op explain how many board members are selected and how votes are distributed. In smaller complexes, the board usually is made up of one or more officers, possibly a president and secretary. In larger complexes, the board may be large enough that it can be subdivided into committees for specific purposes. The important thing to know is that board members are your neighbors and are interested in keeping the value of your property as high as possible. In time, you may even be called to serve. However, that doesn't mean that you and the board will always agree on every issue.

The budget. The main duty of the board is to collect fees and spend the money needed to meet the obligations of the complex. For this purpose, a budget should be prepared and copies distributed to all owners. A projected budget should serve to determine the fees necessary to run the complex for the next year. In co-ops, this amount is called the *cash requirement* and establishes the level of rent or maintenance each resident must pay.

House rules. The board also must enforce the house rules and bring action against residents who violate them. This is one of the more unpleasant duties of board members. Often there is an amount of discretion that must be exercised by the board—for example, when residents request approval of alterations and improvements. In co-ops, the board must interview and approve prospective residents. Performing these duties is made easier if the board can follow a consistent policy as a guide to making decisions. Arbitrary decision making also invites criticism and discontent among residents.

Since the board is so important to your enjoyment of your condo or co-op, it is a good idea to find out beforehand the procedures for dealing with the board. First, familiarize yourself with the bylaws and lease provisions that pertain to board actions and authority. Then talk to board members to get a feel for how things are customarily handled.

44

HOME OWNERSHIP AND INCOME TAXES

You may have heard that you can save on your income taxes if you own a home, but never really understood what this meant. These comments refer to the ability of homeowners to deduct from their taxable income amounts associated with certain expenses of home ownership. This means that, when figured on an after-tax basis, the costs of owning a home are lower than the out-of-pocket expenses. The higher your tax bracket, the more valuable these deductions are. That is one reason why most people with above-average income prefer to own a home.

The major tax benefits stem from two basic expenses—mortgage interest and property taxes. At one time, all types of taxes and interest were deductible, but now mortgage interest and local property taxes are among the few tax deductions individuals can take.

Mortgage interest. When you make your monthly mortgage payment, a portion of the money goes to retiring the principal of the loan and the rest is interest. For the first few years, almost all of the payment is interest and this can be deducted from your taxable income. At the end of the year, the lender will provide you with a breakdown of what you paid during the year so that you can report it on your tax form.

There is a limit of $1 million on the loan used to acquire or improve the home and $100,000 on any additional debt. If your loan exceeds these amounts, interest on the excess is not deductible. This limit may come into play when a loan is refinanced. For example, suppose a home is worth $500,000 and the $200,000 loan balance is refinanced with a loan of $400,000. Of the new loan amount, $200,000 is considered acquisition debt, an additional $100,000 generates deductible interest, and the remaining $100,000 provides no tax deductions. Consequently, the taxpayer could deduct only 75 percent of the total mortgage interest paid. Eligible mortgage interest can be deducted on both a first and second home, but not a third or fourth.

Property tax. There is no limit on the amount of property tax expense that you can claim. These taxes are usually paid out of an escrow account maintained by your lender. The lender pays the bill and reports to you at the end of the year how much was paid. The amount paid to the taxing districts is deductible, not the amount you actually paid into the escrow account. For example, suppose you pay $100 into the escrow account each month for taxes. This amount is based on the lender's estimate of what the tax bill will be. The bill turns out to be $1,100, rather than the $1,200 collected during the year. You deduct only the $1,100 on your tax return and the extra $100 stays in escrow for next year's bill. If the association was late and didn't pay the bill until the following year, the deduction is allowed the next year.

Another advantage is the ability to convert non-deductible consumer interest into tax-deductible mortgage interest. If you own a home and it is worth significantly more than you owe on it, you may be able to take out a home equity loan. Interest on up to $100,000 of home equity debt is deductible, even though the money is not used for housing purposes. You can use the proceeds to pay off other debts, thereby converting nondeductible interest to deductible interest.

The Taxpayer Relief Act. The Taxpayer Relief Act of 1997 brought relief to those who sell homes after May 7, 1997. Specifically, anyone can exclude $250,000 of gain from a sale, and a married couple can exclude $500,000.

This exclusion can be used no more often than once every two years. To be eligible, the seller must have used the property as a principal residence for at least two years within the most recent five years.

This provision replaces both the "rollover" requirement and the $125,000 one-time exclusion for home sellers older than age 55.

IRS Form 2119, once used to report the gain on sale, is no longer used. Sellers who have more than $250,000 profit on a house ($500,000 for married couples) report their gain on Schedule D of IRS Form 1040.

45

CONDO/CO-OP TAX CONSIDERATIONS

The income tax benefits afforded homeowners are fully available to condo and co-op owners. However, you need to know a few things to make sure you get all the deductions you are entitled to.

1. Homeowner tax deductions for condominium owners is basically the same as for any other homeowner. Since you pay mortgage payments directly to the lender, you will receive an accounting for all interest and property taxes paid for the tax year. In addition, if the owners' association has taken out a mortgage loan to finance common area improvements, you can deduct a portion of the interest payments. Calculate your pro rata share of the deductions in the same way that your monthly fee is determined. For example, if the complex has 100 units and everyone pays the same fee, you should deduct 1 percent of the mortgage interest paid by the association. The same is true of any separate property taxes paid by the association.

2. You may be able to deduct discount points paid for getting the loan. Points are deductible if they are considered interest on the loan. Any portion that is considered a fee for granting the loan is not deductible. However, if you paid points to refinance your old mortgage loan, you cannot deduct the payment in the current tax year, but instead may spread the cost over the life of the loan. Consult your tax professional on exactly how to handle these types of deductions.

3. If you own a co-op, you probably do not have a mortgage loan. The type of loan used to buy co-op shares is one secured by your shares of stock. This type of loan generates tax-deductible housing interest. If, instead, you also arranged a signature loan, without giving your home as collateral, it is considered a personal loan. Interest on these types of loans is not deductible.

4. In all likelihood, the co-op has a master mortgage loan secured by the building. If so, you can deduct your pro rata share of the interest paid.

5. You may also deduct your share of property taxes paid by the corporation. Figure your share in the same way that your monthly rent or maintenance fee is determined. Your board should provide you with a report showing your share of deductible expenses.

6. Suppose the condo or co-op is a second home that you rent out when you are not using it. If the period when you rent it out is 14 days or fewer, you need not report the rental income and you can take deductions just as if you had lived there all year. When the rental period exceeds two weeks per year, you have a mixed use property and must report income and expenses for the rental period. (See the next Key for more detail.)

The tax laws make it possible for a person to sell his or her home and buy another without having to pay taxes on any resale profits. This was addressed in the previous Key.

46

TAXATION OF SECOND AND VACATION HOMES

In the previous Key, we covered the tax benefits available to homeowners. These benefits also extend to second or vacation homes. However, if you rent out your home for more than 14 days per year, the rules are more complicated.

Second home. If you rent the property to others for two weeks or less, you may treat it as your residence and you don't have to report the rental income. Generally, you can deduct interest subject to limits of $1 million to acquire two homes, along with local taxes, on these two properties, but not other expenses even though they are attributable to the rental. Another $100,000 of mortgage debt can generate tax-deductible interest.

Vacation home. If your personal use exceeds 14 days, or 10 percent of rental use, whichever is greater, it is considered a vacation home. You must report the rental income as part of your taxable income, but at least some of your maintenance expenses become business deductions. You must allocate expenses between personal and business, typically in the proportion of time used as such. For example, if you use the property half the time and rent it half the time, you can deduct half the interest and taxes as personal itemized deductions and the other half, plus operating expenses and depreciation attributable to rentals, from rental income. You must report all the rental income, but may not claim deductions in excess of rental income.

Here's an example. You rent out a condo for 300 days out of the year and use it personally for the other 65 days. Rental income is $6,000. You pay $5,000 in mortgage interest, $500 in property taxes, $1,000 for insurance and property management, and have $2,500 in depreciation (see your tax advisor to set up a depreciation schedule). The time rented is 82.2 percent of the year, so you can use this percentage of expenses for the rental part:

	Schedule A Itemized deduction	Schedule E Rent income
Rental income received		$ 6,000
Expenses:		
Interest	$ 890	$ 4,110
Property tax	89	411
Repairs: business portion		822
Depreciation: business portion		2,055
Subtotal	$ 979	$ 7,398
Difference, rental income less expenses		$ 1,398
Reduction in allowable depreciation		1,398
Taxable income		0

Note that, even though 82.2 percent of expenses and depreciation is attributable to rental income, a tax loss cannot be generated by a vacation home. Therefore, taxable income is shown as zero. The expenses are deducted in a certain order: first, interest and taxes; second, operating costs; third, depreciation.

It should be noted that the Internal Revenue Service and the Tax Court have used different ratios to determine the proportion of expenses that may be deducted. This difference occurs when total use is less than 365 days, for example when rental use in a year is 30 days and personal use is 70 days. If you are in this situation, consult your tax advisor.

Rental property. Suppose that you seldom use the unit for personal purposes. Personal use not only includes use by you and your family, but any time you rent it out for less than the going rate. If personal use is minimal (less than the greater of 15 days a year or 10 percent of rental use), you cannot claim itemized deductions for interest or taxes. You must report the rental income, and you can deduct operating expenses, interest, and depreciation from this income, on Schedule E of tax Form 1040.

If tax losses are generated, they are called *passive losses* and carry forward to offset future income of the project. Passive losses of less than $25,000 may offset other income, provided you earn less than $100,000 from other sources and actively participate in property management (approve tenants, major expenses). This $25,000 maximum offset is reduced by 50 cents for every dollar above $100,000 that you earn, so owners with more than $150,000 of other income are allowed no offset in the current year for rental property losses. Note that there are certain exemptions to these limitations for real estate professionals.

47

ESTIMATING TOTAL COSTS OF CONDO OWNERSHIP

You can figure the total costs of owning a condo or co-op in the same way that you would a single-family house. The only difference is the monthly assessment for common area maintenance (CAM).

Mortgage. Interest and principal payments on the mortgage loan depend on the amount borrowed, interest rate, and type of loan selected. Mortgage interest rates can fluctuate significantly. Allowing for a typical 30-year mortgage at 8 percent interest, monthly payments are about $7.34 per dollar of the initial loan. That would be $734 per month for a loan principal of $100,000, based on an 80 percent loan on a $125,000 unit.

Taxes. Taxes vary widely depending on the jurisdiction and the exemptions allowed (homestead, elderly). Taxes depend largely on services provided (fire, police) and the schools, including teacher salaries, number of students, class size, and other elements that determine the level of quality. Taxes also depend largely on the commercial and industrial tax base in the community. A strictly "bedroom community" will likely have a higher tax rate than one with a significant amount of taxable business property. A typical effective tax rate in a major metropolitan area is 2 percent of the asset value. This would be $2,500 per year (about $200 per month) for a $125,000 condo.

Insurance. Insurance varies depending largely on hazards in the area (risk of damage from hailstorms or hurricanes, freeze damage, burglary rates). A typical rate is one-half of 1 percent per year, which is $625 for a $125,000 unit, or about $50 per month.

Interior maintenance. A condo or co-op owner is responsible for interior maintenance such as paint, wallpaper, carpet replacement, appliance repairs and replacement, remodeling, and plumbing and electrical repairs within the unit. While this varies greatly, figure at least one-half of 1 percent of the property value per month, which is $50 for a $125,000 unit.

Tax deductions. Interest and property taxes are deductible from federal taxable income. Your savings depends on your tax bracket (maximum of 40 percent) and the deductions provided above the standard deduction.

CAM. CAM for a condo may range from a modest $100 a month to several hundred dollars. It is used to cover grounds maintenance such as mowing and gardening, insurance and taxes on the common areas, exterior painting, structural repairs, clubhouse and swimming pool maintenance and repairs, snow removal, trash collections, security, and management fees. A manager is also needed to look after the property, collect fees, and select and pay contractors.

The amount of CAM depends principally on choices made by the owners' association's management and the general cost of maintenance in your area. You will have a vote in the association and can become more active or vocal than other owners if you really want to influence decisions.

To estimate total monthly costs of ownership, add all the above together.

	Typical Unit $125,000	Your Unit
Interest and principal	$734	
Property taxes	200	
Insurance	50	
Interior maintenance	50	
Common area maintenance	125	
Total monthly cost	$1,159	
Less: Income tax benefit (28% of $800)	224	
Total estimated after-tax monthly cost	$ 935	

48

KEEPING RECORDS

For tax, insurance, financial, and legal reasons, it's important to keep good records on your condo or co-op, especially records concerning its purchase and ownership. These include receipts for money paid on or before the closing, a copy of the mortgage note or deed of trust, your copy of the deed or co-op share certificate, your warranties on the condo or co-op, and any FHA- or VA-related documents.

Insurance records should include a copy of the hazard or homeowner's insurance policy; mortgage, life, or flood insurance policies; and a list of your personal property in the home and its value. Keep records of money spent on maintenance, repairs, and especially home improvements. Photographs of your home and its contents, including closets, will be invaluable when it comes to proving losses for insurance purposes. A good precaution is to put all important papers and photographs in a bank vault. That way they exist even if catastrophe hits your home. You might wish to keep photocopies at home for convenient reference.

It is a good idea to keep a list of valuable records and their location, and to inform your attorney where to find important papers.

In a tax dispute with the IRS, the burden of proof is on the taxpayer. You need to keep the records required to substantiate the tax basis for your residence. If you have sold residences previous to this one, you need to keep records of those prior transactions. Use a worksheet like the one that follows to compute your tax basis and gain or loss on the sale.

Purchase price	_____
Add: Legal and recording fees	_____
Cost of kitchen remodeling	_____
Cost of new windows	_____
Adjusted tax basis	_____

To compute gain upon resale, subtract the adjusted tax basis from the amount realized; the amount realized is the sale price less expenses of sale, as shown below:

Selling price	_____
Less: Broker commission	_____
Loan penalty	_____
Legal and recording	_____
Advertising expenses	_____
Amount realized	_____

Amount realized minus adjusted tax basis is the gain or loss on a sale. See Key 44 for a discussion of taxability.

49

DEALING WITH A DEVELOPER OR A CONVERTER

When you buy a condo or co-op before it is completed or shortly after, you should be mindful of potential problems. A period of transition follows the completion of any real estate project, as the developer turns the building over to the permanent owners. With condos and co-ops, that period can stretch out over a much longer time, since the building must be sold off in pieces to individual homeowners. Complicating the transition is the interplay between a professional and a group of homeowners inexperienced in property management. Furthermore, many condos and co-ops are not new buildings but are converted from existing rental housing. That means the homeowners may be taking on unforeseen physical problems with the older buildings.

Here are some of the problems you may encounter when buying a unit in an incomplete or recently completed (or converted) condo or co-op.

- *Leftover physical problems with the building.* A dishonest building owner may conclude that it is easier to sell a defective building as condo units than as a whole rental building. Even when the problems are disclosed to the buyers, they may turn out to be much worse than revealed by first appearances. It is always a good idea to hire an inspector when you buy a home. In this case, the inspection may have to cover the entire structure. If you can get the developer or converter to provide a warranty, do it. This may provide some security, although it won't protect you from a dishonest seller.

- *Unrealistic projection of monthly fees.* Again, this problem may result from dishonesty, the seller or agent trying to entice you into buying, or from lack of knowledge. Until the first several budgets are established, there is no good indication of what the fees will be, so any projection you get will not be reliable.

- *Holdover management.* If the complex uses a professional manager, he or she will probably be retained when the project first gets turned over to the owners. This raises the possibility of management working in the interest of the old owner or simply not knowing the difference between condo/co-op management and apartment management. If the manager is a holdover, make sure the contract can be broken on short notice. In fact, the association should not assume any long-term unbreakable contracts entered into by the developer unless they are clearly favorable to the homeowners.

- *Developer or converter still in charge.* This situation means the project has not sold out and the developer still owns a substantial number of units. If very few units have sold, the possibility exists that the project won't make it, especially if it is well into the marketing effort. You generally should avoid committing at this stage. However, somebody must buy the first units or no sales will take place. If you are among the first buyers, you should be compensated for the risk involved by getting a reduced price, compared to comparable units elsewhere.

You should also protect yourself by getting a written promise to refund your deposit if the project fails. If you can, check the reputation of the developer to see if he or she is experienced and reliable. If you do not receive a deed at the closing, because the project is incomplete or the construction lender won't release the property, make every effort to get one as soon as possible.

Overall, realize that you are taking a greater risk and that you expect to receive some compensation. If not, move on to a more secure buying opportunity.

50

CONFLICTS AMONG RESIDENTS

We have emphasized the importance of social compatibility among condo and co-op residents. When looking for a new home, consider the social setting as important as the location and features of the unit itself. If the idea of sharing common space with your neighbors bothers you at all, you should probably avoid buying a condo or co-op unit. However, you should be aware that many new subdivisions of detached homes also have common areas, homeowners' associations, and restrictions on the use of private property. Before you buy a home, have your lawyer review the deed and explain any restrictions included.

Social conflict can be one of the biggest headaches of condo/co-op life. You may have lived in an apartment house where one or more tenants didn't fit in and caused trouble. That can happen as well in a condo or co-op. The difference is that you can't move out as easily when you own the unit. In addition, some people become more determined to fight when they feel they are protecting their property.

In general, these are the types of residents that pose the biggest problem for their neighbors.

1. Those who don't understand or are unwilling to accept the limitations of shared property. They see any effort to enforce restrictions as impositions on their property rights. The problems occur when they erect elaborate alterations and the association tries to stop them.

2. The residents who are constantly looking for vio-

lations of the rules, no matter how petty. A certain amount of reasonable tolerance is needed to make shared living work. A stickler for the rules with time on his or her hands can disrupt the whole complex.

3. Animal lovers who don't understand why everyone doesn't appreciate their pet. Unrestrained pets can be a major problem, especially when the pet's owner lives near those who abhor pets.

4. Groups of residents who, for one reason or another, carry on feuds and vendettas among themselves. Some people will go to great lengths to get justice when they feel wronged or taken advantage of. Unfortunately, the entire complex often suffers as well.

5. Nonowner residents who may not share the same interests as owners, since they are not as committed to the property. In addition, nonresident owners may be as big a problem, since they often will resist needed improvements that require higher fees.

To minimize the chance of buying into these problems, there are several things you should do before committing:

- Familiarize yourself with the restrictions and make sure you can live with them. Try to observe life in the complex. If possible, talk to some of the residents and attend a homeowners' meeting.
- Choose a complex where privacy is maximized. Most important is adequate soundproofing between units. Even compatible neighbors will get on each other's nerves when they can hear everything that happens next door.
- Look for bylaws and house rules that are clearly written. Vague rules provide opportunities for conflict and argument.

51

LEASING OR SUBLEASING YOUR UNIT

Most people who buy condo or co-op units do not expect to become landlords, but situations may arise in which you need to rent out your unit. For example, you may need to be away from your unit for an extended period. Many homeowners have found it necessary to lease out their homes in lieu of selling them in a depressed market. By leasing, they hope to ride out the lull until the unit can be sold at a later time.

Many condo and co-op owners don't look favorably on rental tenants in their complex. Perhaps it is a reminder that their homes often physically resemble rental housing and the diminished status afforded this type of housing. At any rate, the owner who leases out his or her unit may earn the disdain of former neighbors.

In condo complexes, there is little the neighbors can do to prevent you from leasing. Each owner is free to sell or lease the unit without interference. You will still be bound by the authority of the board and still be liable for the monthly fee. You may also be held liable for the actions of your tenants.

To lease your condo unit, you should obtain a written preprinted lease form (available in many business supply stores) and find a tenant. Real estate brokers offer their services in finding tenants as well as buyers. The broker may be available to manage the apartment after it is rented, freeing you from this obligation. With most leases, you will pay the condo fee and the tenant will pay utilities. You should investigate getting special absentee owner insurance to cover your liability and possible damages.

If you are planning to sublease your co-op unit, you may run into difficulties. Since co-op boards have much more discretion over who lives in the building, they can discourage or prevent subleasing. Your rights are spelled out in your proprietary lease. Some co-ops simply do not allow subleasing. In others, you may be required to pay a fee to the board that may diminish the rent you receive from the tenant. All co-ops will require permission of the board and possibly approval of a majority of shareholders. In addition, the tenant must pass an interview with the board.

If you live in a condo, you may consider leasing as an alternative to selling in a slow market. If you have a co-op unit, that option may not be available. Before doing anything, check your lease and consult the board.

52

SELLING YOUR UNIT

If you have sold a home before, you should find that selling your condo or co-op unit is very similar. However, you may be subject to some restrictions that don't apply to detached homes.

If you have never sold a home, it is helpful to review the basic home-selling process. Using the services of a broker will simplify the process, but you should be aware of the steps required. Of course, you have some insight into what it requires to sell a home by having been involved as a buyer. You may not have been aware of what the seller had to do to bring about the sale. This is the general home-selling process:

1. *Preparing for the market.* You have made the decision to sell and may have made a commitment to move, so there is some time pressure on your ability to sell. You should make the home as presentable to buyers as possible. This usually entails minor repairs and cosmetic improvements. Be sure to keep all records of expenses for income tax purposes. Decide on whether you wish to use a broker (see Key 53) and set an appropriate asking price.
2. *Advertising.* You will need to inform the public of the unit's availability. You might run an ad in the newspaper and put out a sign. Also helpful is preparation of a fact sheet that states the unit's features and emphasizes any advantages that may exist.
3. *Showing.* Once you have generated some interest, you will need to give prospective buyers a chance to see the unit. This means setting up appointments

to show the unit and conducting tours of the unit.

4. *Negotiation.* Hopefully, exposure to the market will generate some offers. You should make arrangements to provide prospective buyers with contract forms. This allows you and the buyer to come to agreement, not only on the price but on all aspects of the transaction, and sets up the stage for a completed sale.

5. *Closing.* After a contract is signed and the buyer is arranging financing, you will need to prepare for the closing. A title or abstract company is often helpful in researching title to show it is clear and in providing title insurance. Also, there may be repairs required as a result of the buyer's inspection. At the closing, buyer, seller, lender, their legal representatives, and often title company personnel exchange money and documents to finalize the transition. The closing ends the sales process.

Restrictions. Several restrictions may apply to your ability to sell your unit. In both condos and co-ops, you may not be able to place for sale signs in common areas. In co-ops, the new owner must be approved by the board following an interview. This can be a stumbling block to a sale, depending on how particular the board is in approving residents.

Fair market price. In some cases, there are special requirements that can severely limit your ability to sell at the best price for your unit. Some associations and boards have the right to require you to offer the unit to the board prior to selling it on the market. Along with this right is the stipulation that the price be some "fair market price" set by the board, although the price may be lower than you could obtain in the market. Even if the board declines, it may delay your marketing by several months. In addition, some boards can require you to pay them a portion of any profit you receive from the sale. This could cut severely into the funds you can use to purchase another home. Check your bylaws and condo deed or your proprietary lease and stock shares for any mention of these requirements. If they exist, you may wish to reconsider your decision to sell.

53

SELLER'S USE
OF A BROKER

The majority of home sales are arranged through real estate brokerage companies. While there is no legal restraint on your right to sell your own home, most sellers choose to employ a broker for the following reasons:

1. Brokers are knowledgeable about the current market and the home-selling procedure.
2. Brokers perform most of the work of advertising and showing the property, thus freeing sellers to go about their normal functions.
3. Brokers are often more effective in locating willing buyers quickly.

If you do use a broker, you will probably have to enter into a listing agreement in which the broker will have the exclusive right to sell the home during the listing period—normally three to six months. This means that if you happen to find a buyer on your own, you still owe the broker a commission. Commissions are based on a certain percentage of the sales price and are the responsibility of the seller. The broker earns a commission upon delivering a buyer who is ready, willing, and able to buy at the seller's terms. If the buyer is turned down for financing and this ends the deal, you don't pay a commission. However, if for some reason you pull out of the transaction, the commission is still required.

Here are some of the things a broker can help you with during the selling process.

- *Pricing.* Knowledgeable brokers know what comparable homes have been selling for and can suggest a proper listing price. This can be important, since too low a price cuts into your profits and too high a price can delay the sale.

- *Exposing the property.* The broker will advertise your home. Furthermore, he or she can expose the home in ways not available to you. An *open house* may be conducted to familiarize other brokers with the listing. Your home may be put on the Multiple Listing Service where it will be seen by other brokers in the network. This maximizes the chance that a buyer will see your home.
- *Showing.* The broker will conduct tours of the home. This is especially valuable if you no longer occupy the home. The broker will work with prospective buyers before they visit the property to make sure the home is something they are interested in and can afford to buy. This helps to limit the inspections to the more serious buyers.
- *Assisting in negotiations.* The broker will have approved contract forms and can help buyers in preparing an offer. The broker may act to convey offers and counteroffers between the seller and buyer to speed negotiations. Brokers often act as escrow agents for earnest money deposits as well.
- *Helping prepare for closing.* Agents work with buyers after a contract is signed to help them obtain financing and accomplish the things that must be done before closing. They can also advise the seller on what needs to be done to make sure the closing is completed on time.

Using a broker costs money in the form of a commission. However, a good broker can save you a great deal of trouble and may make the difference in facilitating a successful sale both for the seller and the buyer.

54

SELLER FINANCING

Sometimes, affordable home financing is hard to find, particularly for condo and co-op units. If you are trying to sell during one of these periods you may find few buyers who can manage the purchase. When condo or co-op financing is hard to arrange or when interest rates are high, consider financing the sale yourself.

Seller financing means that some or all of the sales price of the unit consists of a loan from the seller to the buyer. You will be serving as the lender for the buyer. When you do this, you can structure the financing any way you and the buyer agree on. You can lower the interest rate in exchange for getting your price for the unit. Two words of caution are in order:

1. You should avoid providing financing to a buyer who can't get a bank loan because of a bad credit rating. Such buyers are probably looking for someone to take advantage of. Don't let it be you.
2. Try to avoid "no down payment" deals. If the buyer has no money tied up in the property, he or she could walk away at the first sign of trouble. Foreclosure is an expensive and slow process.

Seller financing can be the only loan on the property—a first mortgage in the case of condos—or it can be a junior mortgage that is supplemental to other loans. You can also make the loan subject to a balloon payment. This means the money has to be paid back in full at some point before the loan amortizes. By using a balloon payment, you provide temporary relief from high-cost financing and limit your exposure to risk.

First loan. If you make a first loan, you will have to retire any debt currently on the property; then a portion of the price received will be in the form of a promissory note and mortgage (in the case of a condo; a co-op loan should be secured by pledging the co-op shares). For example, consider a condo unit that is sold for $150,000. The terms of sale are $50,000 in cash and $100,000 in new first mortgage note. The seller has an existing loan with a balance of $60,000. The seller must first pay off the old loan balance using all of the down payment plus $10,000 of his or her own cash.

Second loan. A second loan provided by the seller can be used to reduce the cash down payment required of the buyer. Let's refer to the above example again to illustrate some variations of a second loan. Suppose the old loan of $60,000 can be assumed by the buyer but the buyer doesn't have $90,000 cash to complete the deal. Part of the difference is provided by a second loan. The buyer assumes the $60,000 old loan, provides $20,000 in cash, and gives the seller a $70,000 second mortgage.

Wraparound loan. Another variation is the wraparound loan. In the example, the seller keeps the old $60,000 loan and continues to make the payments; this must be approved by the lender if the seller no longer holds title to the property. The buyer gives $20,000 in cash and gives the seller a $130,000 wraparound mortgage. The seller uses the payments from the buyer to make the payments on the old loan. Thus, if the buyer does not make payments, the seller is faced with the necessity of using his or her own money to keep the loan current.

If the old loan is not assumable or has unfavorable terms compared to new financing, a new loan could be used. In the example, the buyer gets a new first mortgage of $100,000 but doesn't have enough cash for the down payment. The seller takes $20,000 in cash with the difference made up by a $30,000 second mortgage loan from the seller.

Minimizing default. The two biggest problems with providing seller financing are the risk of the buyer defaulting on the loan and the fact that you are getting your money over a long period of time rather than immediately. To minimize the risk of default, you should take steps to properly qualify the buyer. One good way to do this is to arrange with a mortgage lender to do the underwriting for a fee. The lender will use all the proper legal forms to protect your interests. If you need to have the money right away, perhaps to buy your new home, it may be possible to sell the loan to an investor. Check for ads in your local paper for people who buy mortgage loans. Be aware that they won't pay you the face value of the loan. Depending on how creditworthy the borrower is and how the terms of the loan compare to the market, the loan will be discounted in the sale. That means you will get less than its face value in cash.

55

TERMINATING A CONDO OR CO-OP

Many condominiums and co-ops were converted from rental housing. In recent years, there has been a reverse trend, where condos and co-ops have reverted to rental properties. In some areas, the market for rental housing units is stronger than that for home sales and the best use for many apartment complexes may be as rental units.

Evidence that this is happening in your area would be a trend toward absentee owners in your building or complex. When this practice becomes widespread, it is probably time for the complex to convert back to rental. Renting out individual units is inefficient for the owners since there can be no economy of scale in managing the units. It is also unpleasant for the remaining occupant-owners because of potential conflicts between the interests of owners and rental tenants.

In these situations, it might be better if the entire complex were converted. There may be an opportunity to sell the complex to one investor to operate as a rental project. Co-ops generally have a provision that allows the termination of all proprietary leases upon the affirmative vote of a super-majority (two-thirds or three-fourths) of the owners. Check your lease for mention of the conditions for terminating leases. In most condos, any sale of the entire complex would require a sales agreement with each owner. However, in some areas, it is possible to arrange the sale of the whole complex with approval of some specified percentage of owners. Consult an attorney to see if this applies in your area.

There are other ways a condo or co-op project may be

terminated. For example, destruction of all or a large proportion of the building combined with the decision not to rebuild would make continuation of the condo/co-op arrangement impractical. Condemnation of the building by the government would, of course, end its status as a condo or co-op.

If your complex is converted, there is little you can do but go along with it. You will receive your share of the compensation provided from the sale, insurance settlement, or condemnation award. As a condo or co-op owner, you should be aware that a possibility exists that someday your ownership may end through no action of your own.

QUESTIONS AND ANSWERS

What is the difference between owning and living in a condominium or cooperative building and owning and living in any other type of home?

All condominiums and cooperative housing involve some sharing of space with other residents. How much sharing takes place depends on the design of the complex. In condominium town houses, residents share the walls between units and the grounds; in high-rise buildings, most of the structure is shared. Because of this arrangement, condominium and cooperative owners do not have undivided ownership rights to the entire property. In practical terms, this means all owners must comply with certain restrictions on how they can use their property. The arrangement is much like a small community with its own governing body selected by the unit owners.

How is a co-op different from a condo?

When you buy an apartment in a condominium complex, you actually own a portion of the complex in fee simple. In many cases, that portion is defined by the interior boundaries of your unit. Everything else is owned in common with the other unit owners. Cooperative housing is a very different arrangement. The entire complex is owned by a special corporation. When you buy into the co-op, you are purchasing shares in the corporation that entitle you to use of a particular dwelling unit in the complex. In practical terms, the difference is that the governing board of the co-op has much more authority over how you use your property than does the owners' association of a condominium. In addition, you can't finance the purchase of a co-op with a mortgage loan since you have no real property to mortgage. However, you may be able to deduct mortgage interest and property tax expenses from your income taxes like any other homeowner.

If your ownership rights are subject to limitation, why would anyone want to buy a condominium or co-op unit?

There are several reasons why some people are attracted to this type of housing. First of all, the units may be the most affordable housing available. By saving on land costs and a common structure, developers can produce these units less expensively. Second, since less land is required, condos and co-ops can be built in locations where land is expensive. This means that some luxury units are located close to important employment and shopping areas, such as in Manhattan. Third, some are attracted by the ability to own a home without having to do housing chores. Finally, some people like the security or social interaction offered by living close to their neighbors.

What are the most important considerations when buying a condo or co-op unit?

The most important is deciding if you can be comfortable living within the social environment of the complex. Remember that, unlike renting an apartment, you can't readily move away if you don't like your neighbors. Conflicts among residents can make condo/co-op living unbearable. It is also important to check the bylaws or proprietary lease to see if you are allowed to do the things you like to do. Other considerations are the same as for any home: Can you afford the price? Can you get financing? Is the unit structurally sound? Does it have what you need? Will it make a good investment?

Who takes care of running the complex?

In every condo or co-op there is an organization to oversee the areas held in common by all owners. In a co-op, this is the corporation's board of directors. In a condo, it is the owners' association executive board. Either may be referred to as the operating board. Each owner has a voice in selecting these groups and settling questions of policy. The actions of the board are governed by the bylaws of the condo/co-op. The board is authorized to collect a regular fee from each owner to fund the operations of the complex. These boards are made up of individual owners, generally serving without pay. Larger complexes may employ professional property managers to assist the board.

Can you buy condo or co-op units as investments?

Many condo units and some co-op units are owned by investors who rent them out to tenants. This allows an investor to own rental property with a comparatively modest investment. However, several factors may limit investment opportunities. First, in normal markets, condos sell at higher prices than similar rental units; therefore, investors usually buy only in depressed markets. Second, most co-ops and some condos have restrictions on leasing units to nonowners that make investment impractical. Third, some complexes have restrictions on the sale of units. Any investor must carefully check out the restrictions on use of units before buying.

What should I know before buying a condo as a second or vacation home?

The key to buying a second home is deciding how you intend to use it. If you intend to use the condo frequently throughout the year, you will need to purchase a unit strictly as a second home. However, if your use will be confined to a specific period of time, you may want to buy a timeshare. Timeshares allow you the right to a specific unit for a specific time of year. The unit is owned and used by others during the rest of the year. If you own a condo for the whole year, but use it infrequently, you will need to rent it out for the remainder of the year. Some resort condos are set up to help you do this. In addition, you may be able to get some landlord tax benefits, depending on how long you use the unit as compared to renting it out.

Can I finance the purchase of a condo or co-op like any other home?

In the case of a condo, the answer is yes. You can get mortgage financing for your unit from almost any mortgage lender. However, lenders may be reluctant to provide mortgage loans for condos when sales are down and there have been a lot of foreclosures. Check on loan availability and terms before committing to buy. Co-op financing is a different situation. Since you are actually buying shares in a corporation, rather than real property, you can't use a mortgage loan to buy the shares. If co-ops are popular in your area, there may be special financing based on the security provided by your share certificates. The interest you pay is tax-deductible, as is the case with a mortgage loan, and if the cooperative has its own mortgage loan on the building, you can deduct your proportional share of mortgage interest expense. You can get FHA insurance, which allows you to reduce the cash down payment, to cover loans for condos through the 234(c) program, and for co-ops through the 203(n) program.

I live in an apartment building that is being converted into a condominium. What should I do?

First, decide whether you want to move or not. If you

don't want to buy or can't afford to buy and don't mind moving, find out if the converter has set aside funds for moving expenses. If you want to keep your apartment, there may be a way to stay. The converter may sell some units to investors who will continue to rent them out. However, your rent may be raised.

Most likely, if you want to stay, you will have to buy your apartment. Often, converters offer reduced prices to current tenants and may have special financing as well. Find out what your options are and try to take the course that is best for you.

Why do I have to pay a monthly fee?

Monthly fees are necessary to pay the expenses of running the complex. In a condo, these expenses may include utilities and maintenance of the common areas, management fees, and insurance. A co-op will have these same expenses, plus property taxes and payments on any mortgage loan used to acquire the building. As an owner, you are entitled to see the operating budget for the complex.

Failure to pay these fees can have dire consequences. A condo association may place a lien on a delinquent owner's unit and force it to be sold for back payments. The co-op board can cancel your lease and reissue your stock upon default on your obligation.

What kind of insurance do I need?

In most cases, the condo association or co-op board will carry liability and hazard insurance on the property. However, that probably will not be thorough coverage. It will definitely not cover your personal property and may not cover anything inside your unit. There are special policies designed for condo and co-op owners that are intended to fill in these gaps. If this type of policy is not available in your area, you may be able to get by with a renter's policy.

Who handles repairs when they are needed?

Technically, most repairs are the responsibility of the condo association or co-op corporation. In practice, there is probably a dividing line between what is the duty of the group and what is your responsibility. In emergencies, you may be able to have the repairs done and get reimbursed.

Many owners take care of repairs themselves and don't bother the board, figuring that to be the most convenient way to get it done. On big repairs, especially involving structural components, you may need to consult with the board as they may have procedures on how the job must be done.

Suppose I want to make alterations to my unit?

Altering the appearance or function of a unit may be severely restricted by the bylaws of the condo or co-op. Minor remodeling of the interior of the unit is probably no problem. Changes such as painting the exterior a different color, adding an antenna, or converting a garage would probably need approval from the board before the work is done. If you fail to follow procedures, the board may be able to force you to return the unit to its original condition.

I'm going to be out of the country next year. Will I be able to lease out my apartment?

Most co-ops and some condos place restrictions on your ability to lease your unit. The fear is that the complex will become populated with rental tenants who are viewed as more transient and less concerned about property condition than are resident owners. If there are restrictions, you will need to gain approval from the board. If you live in a co-op, your tenants may have to pass an interview with the board, just as you did when you moved in.

What do I need to know before I try to sell my unit?

First, find out if the board places any restrictions on sales of units. Some complexes give the board the right to acquire units before anyone else can buy them or require the seller to surrender a portion of resale profits. Next, find out how units are selling and if financing is available. You should consider if you want to try to sell the unit yourself or use a broker. Brokers work on commission, so if they can't sell your unit, you don't owe them anything.

GLOSSARY

Many of the following terms were adapted from the *Real Estate Handbook* or the *Dictionary of Real Estate Terms*, published by Barron's Educational Series; all rights reserved.

A

Acceptance   agreeing to take an offer.

Acre   a measure of land containing 43,560 square feet.

Ad valorem tax   a tax based on the value of the property.

Adjustable-rate mortgage (ARM)   one where the interest rate fluctuates according to another rate, as when the mortgage rate is adjusted annually based on the one-year Treasury bill rate, plus a 2 percent margin.

Agency   the legal relationship between a principal and his or her agent arising from a contract in which the principal engages the agent to perform certain acts on the principal's behalf.

Agent   one who undertakes to transact some business or to manage some affair for another, with the authority of the latter.

Agency disclosure a written form that announces whether the state-licensed broker in a transaction represents the buyer or the seller.

Agreement of sale   a written agreement between buyer and seller to transfer real estate at a future date. Includes all the conditions required for a sale.

Amortization   a gradual process of reducing a debt in a systematic manner.

Appraisal   an expert's opinion of the value of property arrived at with careful consideration of all available and relevant data.

Appreciation   increase in the value of property.

As is   the present condition of property. The "as is" clause is likely to warn of a defect.

Assessed value   the value against which a property tax is imposed. The assessed value is often lower than the market value due to state law, conservative tax district appraisals, and infrequent appraisals.

Assignment   the method by which a right or contract is transferred from one person to another.

Assumable mortgage   one that can be transferred to another party. The transferee assumes the debt but the original borrower is not released from the debt without a novation.

B

Balloon mortgage   a loan having a large final payment.

Balloon payment   the final payment on a debt.

Binder   a brief agreement showing intent to follow with a formal contract.

Board   see *operating board*.

Broker   one who is licensed by a state to act for property owners or buyers in real estate transactions, within the scope of state law.

Buyer's broker   a state-licensed real estate broker whose role it is to obtain the best arrangements for the prospective buyer whom he or she represents.

Bylaws   an official document that states how the condominium association or co-op operating board is set up, its duties, and the rights and obligations of unit or share owners.

C

CAM   an acronym for common area maintenance. A condo or co-op owner must pay a proportionate share of common area maintenance, including lawn service, insurance, taxes, and repairs to walkways, fences, and the like.

Cap   the maximum rate of change of interest rate of an adjustable-rate mortgage. The mortgage may have an annual or lifetime ceiling.

Capital gain   gain on the sale of a capital asset. If long-term (generally over six months), capital gains are sometimes favorably taxed. A personal residence is a capital asset.

Caveat emptor   "Let the buyer beware." An expression once used in real estate to put the burden of an undisclosed defect on the buyer. This concept has been eroded in most states.

Closing   the date when buyer and seller exchange money for property.

Closing costs   various fees and expenses payable by the seller and buyer at the time of a real estate closing (also termed *transaction costs*). Included are brokerage commissions, discount points, title insurance and examination, deed recording fees, and appraisal fees.

Closing statement   an accounting of funds from a real estate sale, made to both the seller and the buyer separately. Most states require the broker to furnish accurate closing statements to all parties to the transaction.

Cloud on title   an outstanding claim or encumbrance that, if valid, would affect or impair the owner's title.

Commission   **1.** an amount earned by a real estate broker for his or her services. **2.** the official state agency that enforces real estate licensing laws.

Commitment letter   a written pledge or promise; a firm agreement, often used to describe the terms of a mortgage loan that is being offered.

Common elements   in a condominium, those portions of the property not owned individually by unit owners but in which an indivisible interest is held by all unit owners. Generally includes the grounds, parking areas, recreational facilities, and external structure of the building.

Conditional sales contract   a contract for the sale of property stating that the seller retains title until the conditions of the contract have been fulfilled. See *contract for deed*.

Condominium a system of ownership of individual units in a multiunit structure, combined with joint ownership of commonly used property (sidewalks, hallways, stairs, etc.). See *common elements*.

Consideration anything of value given to induce entering into a contract; it may be money, personal services, or love and affection.

Contingency a condition that must be satisfied before the party to a contract must purchase or sell.

Contract an agreement between competent parties to do or not to do certain things for a consideration. Common real estate contracts are contract of sale, contract for deed, mortgage, lease, listing, deed.

Contract for deed a real estate installment sales arrangement whereby the buyer may use, occupy, and enjoy land, but no deed is given by the seller (so no title passes) until all or a specified part of the sale price has been paid. Same as *land contract, installment land contract, conditional sales contract.*

Contract of sale same as *agreement of sale.*

Conventional loan, mortgage **1.** a mortgage loan other than one guaranteed by the Veterans Administration or insured by the Federal Housing Administration. See *VA loan, FHA loan* **2.** A fixed-rate, fixed-term mortgage loan.

Conversion process of creating a condominium or cooperative housing from rental housing. Primarily a legal and marketing process, but may involve some renovation and remodeling of the building.

Cooperative a type of corporate ownership of real property whereby stockholders of the corporation are entitled to use a certain dwelling unit or other units of space. Special income tax laws allow the tenant stockholders to deduct interest and property taxes paid by the corporation.

D

Declaration of condominium the legal document that establishes a property under condominium ownership.

Deed a written document, properly signed and delivered, that conveys title to real property. See *general warranty deed, quitclaim deed, special warranty deed.*

Deed of trust   an instrument used in many states in lieu of a mortgage. Legal title to the property is vested in one or more trustees to secure the repayment of the loan.

Deed restriction   a clause in a deed that limits the use of land.

Default   failure to fulfill an obligation or promise, or to perform specified acts.

Deficiency judgment   a court order stating that the borrower still owes money when the security for a loan does not entirely satisfy a defaulted debt.

Depreciation   a deduction against taxable income from rental property to account for the gradual loss in value of a structure. This deduction is not available for owner-occupied housing.

Discount points   amounts paid to the lender (often by the seller) at the time of origination of a loan, to account for the difference between market interest rate and the lower face rate of the note.

Down payment   the amount one pays for property in addition to the debt incurred.

Due-on-sale clause   a provision in a mortgage that states that the loan is due upon sale of the property.

E

Earnest money   a deposit made before closing by a purchaser of real estate to evidence good faith.

Easement   the right, privilege, or interest that one party has in the land of another. The most common easements are for utility lines.

Encumbrance   any right to or interest in land that affects its value. Includes outstanding mortgage loans, unpaid taxes, easements, and deed restrictions.

Equity   the interest or value that the owner has in real estate over and above the liens against it.

Equity loan   usually a second mortgage whereby the property owner borrows against the house, based on the value of equity built up by appreciation.

Escrow an agreement between two or more parties providing that certain instruments or property be placed with a third party for safekeeping, pending the fulfillment or performance of some act or condition.

Exclusive agency listing employment contract giving only one broker, for a specified time, the right to sell the property and also allowing the owner alone to sell the property without paying a commission.

Exclusive right to sell listing employment contract giving the broker the right to collect commission if the property is sold by anyone, including the owner, during the term of the agreement. See also *multiple listing service.*

Execute to sign a contract; sometimes, to perform a contract fully.

F

Fair market value a term, generally used in property tax and condemnation legislation, meaning the market value of the property.

Federal Fair Housing Law a federal law that forbids discrimination on the basis of race, color, sex, religion, national origin, handicap, or familial status in the selling or renting of homes and apartments.

Federal Housing Administration (FHA) an agency within the U.S. Department of Housing and Urban Development that administers many loan programs, loan guarantee programs, and loan insurance programs designed to make more housing available.

Fee simple, fee absolute absolute ownership of real property; owner is entitled to the entire property with unconditional power of disposition during his or her life, and it descends to the heirs and legal representatives upon the owner's death intestate.

FHA loan a mortgage loan insured by the FHA.

First mortgage a mortgage that has priority as a lien over all other mortgages. In cases of foreclosure, the first mortgage will be satisfied before other mortgages.

Fixed-rate mortgage one on which the interest rate does not change over the entire term of the loan.

Fixtures personal property attached to the land or improvements so as to become part of the real estate.

Foreclosure a termination of all rights of a mortgagor or the grantee in the property covered by the mortgage.

G

General warranty deed a deed in which the grantor agrees to protect the grantee against any other claim to title to the property and provides other promises.

Graduated-payment mortgage (GPM) a mortgage requiring lower payments in early years than in later years. Payments increase in steps each year until the installments are sufficient to amortize the loan.

Grantee the party to whom the title to real property is conveyed; the buyer.

Grantor anyone who gives a deed.

H

Hazard insurance a form of insurance that protects against certain risks, such as fires and storms.

Homeowners' association an organization of the homeowners in a particular subdivision, planned unit development, or condominium; generally for the purpose of enforcing deed restrictions or managing the common elements of the development.

Homeowner's policy an insurance policy designed especially for homeowners. Usually protects the owner from losses caused by most common disasters, theft, and liability. Coverage and costs vary widely.

House rules an addendum to a co-op proprietary lease or condominium bylaws that states restrictions on the use of property in the complex.

J

Joint tenancy ownership of realty by two or more persons, each of whom has an undivided interest with the right of survivorship.

Junior mortgage a mortgage whose claim against the property will be satisfied only after prior mortgages have been repaid. See *first mortgage.*

L

Land contract same as *contract for deed.*

Lien a charge against property making it security for the payment of a debt, judgment, mortgage, or taxes; it is a type of encumbrance. A specific lien is against certain property only. A general lien is against all the property owned by the debtor.

List to give or obtain a listing.

Listing 1. a written engagement contract between a principal and an agent, authorizing the agent to perform services for the principal involving the latter's property. **2.** a record of property for sale by a broker who has been authorized by the owner to sell. **3.** the property so listed.

Listing agreement, listing contract same as *listing* (1).

Loan-to-value ratio (LTV) the portion of the amount borrowed compared to the cost or value of the property purchased.

M

Maintenance term often applied to the monthly fee charged co-op owners to pay for building expenses. May also be called rent.

Market value the most probable price a buyer, willing but not compelled to buy, would pay, and the price a seller, willing but not compelled to sell, would accept.

Mechanic's lien a lien given by law upon a building or other improvement upon land, and upon the land itself, as security for the payment for labor done and materials furnished for improvement.

Mortgage a written instrument that creates a lien upon real estate as security for the payment of a specified debt.

Mortgagee one who holds a lien on property or title to property, as security for a debt; the lender.

Mortgagor   one who pledges property as security for a loan; the borrower.

Mortgage banker   one who originates, sells, and services mortgage loans. Most loans are insured or guaranteed by a government agency or private mortgage insurer.

Mortgage insurance   protection for the lender in the event of default, usually covering 10 to 20 percent of the amount borrowed.

Multiple Listing Service (MLS)   an association of real estate brokers that agrees to share listings with one another. The listing broker and the selling broker share the commission. The MLS usually distributes a book with all listings to its members, updating the book frequently. Prospective buyers benefit from the ability to select from among many homes listed by any member broker.

N

Negative amortization   an increase in the outstanding balance of a loan resulting from the failure of periodic debt service payments to cover required interest charged on the loan.

Net listing   a listing in which the broker's commission is the excess of the sales price over an agreed-upon (net) price to the seller; illegal in some states.

Notary public   an officer who is authorized to take acknowledgments to certain types of documents, such as deeds, contracts, and mortgages, and before whom affidavits may be sworn.

O

Offer   an expression of willingness to purchase a property at a specified price.

Open house   a method of showing a home for sale whereby the home is left open for inspection by interested parties.

Open housing   a condition under which housing units may be purchased or leased without regard for racial, ethnic, color, religious, handicap, or familial characteristics of the buyers or tenants.

Open listing a listing given to any number of brokers without liability to compensate any except the one who first secures a buyer who is ready, willing, and able to meet the terms of the listing or secures the seller's acceptance of another offer. The sale of the property automatically terminates all open listings.

Operating board the decision-making and executive group for the cooperative or condominium association. Members are generally elected by the owners and serve limited terms.

Oral contract an unwritten agreement. With few exceptions, oral agreements for the sale or use of real estate are unenforceable. In most states, contracts for the sale or rental of real estate, unless they are in writing, are unenforceable under the Statute of Frauds. Oral leases for a year or less are often acceptable.

P

Permanent mortgage a mortgage for a long period of time (over 10 years).

Plat a plan or map of a specific land area.

Points see *discount points*.

Prepayment penalty a penalty imposed on a borrower when a loan is retired before maturity.

Prepayment privilege the right of a borrower to retire a loan before maturity.

Principal **1.** one who owns or will use property. **2.** one who contracts for the services of an agent or broker; the broker's or agent's client. **3.** the amount of money raised by a mortgage or other loan, as distinct from the interest paid on it.

Principal and interest (P&I) payment a periodic payment, usually made monthly, that includes the interest charges for the period plus an amount applied to amortization of the principal balance. Commonly used with self-amortizing loans.

Principal, interest, taxes, and insurance (PITI)   the monthly mortgage payment (P&I), with the addition of an amount deposited in escrow for future payment of taxes and insurance.

Private mortgage insurance (PMI)   see *mortgage insurance*.

Profit turnback   In some complexes, the right of the operating board to share in the profits realized when a unit is sold.

Proprietary lease   a document that establishes the right to occupy an apartment within cooperative housing, along with the conditions and limitations on the use of the property.

Prorate   to allocate between seller and buyer their proportionate share of an obligation paid or due; for example, to prorate real estate taxes.

Purchase money mortgage   a mortgage given by a grantee (buyer) to a grantor (seller) in part payment of the purchase price of real estate.

Q

Quitclaim deed   a deed that conveys only the grantor's rights or interest in real estate, without stating the nature of the rights and with no warranties of ownership. Often used to remove a possible cloud on the title. Contrast with *general warranty deed*.

R

Real estate   1. in law, land and everything more or less attached to it. Ownership below to the center of the earth and above to the heavens. Distinguished from *personal property*. Same as *realty*. **2.** in business, the activities concerned with ownership and use transfers of the physical property.

Real Estate Settlement Procedures Act (RESPA)   a law that states how mortgage lenders must treat those who apply for federally related real estate loans on property with one to four dwelling units. Intended to provide borrowers with more knowledge when they comparison shop for mortgage money.

Refinance to substitute a new loan for an old one, often in order to borrow more or reduce the interest rate.

Right of first refusal in some complexes, the right of the operating board to buy, at some stated value, a unit before it is put on the open market.

S

Sales contract same as *contract of sale*.

Self-amortizing mortgage one that will retire itself through regular principal and interest payments. Contrast with *balloon mortgage*.

Seller's market economic conditions that favor sellers, reflecting rising prices and market activity.

Settlement same as *closing*.

Special assessment any charge levied on unit owners in addition to the regular monthly fee. Such assessments are used generally to pay for emergency or unusual repairs or improvements.

Special warranty deed a deed in which the grantor limits the title warranty given to the grantee to anyone claiming by, from, through, or under him, the grantor. The grantor does not warrant against title defects arising from conditions that existed before he owned the property.

Stigma a negative perception of a property that has been contaminated, which continues after remediation.

Subject to mortgage a buyer taking title to mortgaged real property but not personally responsible for the payment of any portion of the amount due. The buyer must make payments in order to keep the property; however, if the buyer fails to do so, only his or her equity in that property is lost.

Survey the process by which a parcel of land is measured and its area ascertained; also, the blueprint showing the measurements, boundaries, and area.

T

Term, amortization for a loan, the period of time during which principal and interest payments must be made; generally, the time needed to amortize the loan fully.

Title evidence that the owner of the land is in lawful possession thereof; evidence of ownership.

Title insurance an insurance policy that protects the holder from loss sustained by defects in the title.

Title search an examination of the public records to determine the ownership and encumbrances affecting real property.

V

Veterans Administration (VA) a government agency that provides certain services to discharged servicemen.

VA loan, mortgage one that is guaranteed by the United States Veterans Administration. Discharged servicemen with more than 120 days of active duty are generally eligible for a VA loan, which typically does not require a down payment.

Vendee buyer.

Vendor seller.

W

Warranty deed title to real estate in which the grantor guarantees title. Usually protects against other claimants, liens, or encumbrances and offers good title.

PAYMENT TABLES

**Monthly Principal and Interest Payments
per $1,000 of Principal**

Term (Years)	Contract Interest Rate (%)			
	5.00	**5.25**	**5.50**	**5.75**
1	85.61	85.73	85.84	85.96
2	43.88	43.99	44.10	44.21
3	29.98	30.09	30.20	30.31
4	23.03	23.15	23.26	23.38
5	18.88	18.99	19.11	19.22
6	16.11	16.23	16.34	16.46
7	14.14	14.26	14.37	14.49
8	12.66	12.78	12.90	13.02
9	11.52	11.64	11.76	11.89
10	10.61	10.73	10.86	10.98
11	9.87	9.99	10.12	10.24
12	9.25	9.38	9.51	9.63
13	8.74	8.86	8.99	9.12
14	8.29	8.42	8.55	8.68
15	7.91	8.04	8.18	8.31
16	7.58	7.71	7.85	7.98
17	7.29	7.43	7.56	7.70
18	7.04	7.17	7.31	7.45
19	6.81	6.94	7.08	7.22
20	6.60	6.74	6.88	7.03
21	6.42	6.56	6.70	6.85
22	6.26	6.40	6.54	6.69
23	6.11	6.25	6.40	6.54
24	5.97	6.12	6.27	6.41
25	5.85	6.00	6.15	6.30
26	5.74	5.89	6.04	6.19
27	5.64	5.78	5.94	6.09
28	5.54	5.69	5.84	6.00
29	5.45	5.61	5.76	5.92
30	5.37	5.53	5.68	5.84

Monthly Principal and Interest Payments
per $1,000 of Principal

Term (Years)	Contract Interest Rate (%)			
	6.00	6.25	6.50	6.75
1	86.07	86.19	86.30	86.42
2	44.33	44.44	44.55	44.66
3	30.43	30.54	30.65	30.77
4	23.49	23.60	23.72	23.84
5	19.34	19.45	19.57	19.69
6	16.58	16.70	16.81	16.93
7	14.61	14.73	14.85	14.98
8	13.15	13.27	13.39	13.51
9	12.01	12.13	12.26	12.38
10	11.11	11.23	11.36	11.49
11	10.37	10.50	10.63	10.76
12	9.76	9.89	10.02	10.16
13	9.25	9.38	9.52	9.65
14	8.82	8.95	9.09	9.22
15	8.44	8.58	8.72	8.85
16	8.12	8.26	8.40	8.54
17	7.84	7.98	8.12	8.26
18	7.59	7.73	7.87	8.01
19	7.37	7.51	7.65	7.80
20	7.17	7.31	7.46	7.61
21	6.99	7.14	7.29	7.44
22	6.84	6.98	7.13	7.29
23	6.69	6.84	7.00	7.15
24	6.56	6.72	6.87	7.03
25	6.45	6.60	6.76	6.91
26	6.34	6.50	6.65	6.81
27	6.24	6.40	6.56	6.72
28	6.16	6.31	6.48	6.64
29	6.07	6.24	6.40	6.56
30	6.00	6.16	6.33	6.49

Monthly Principal and Interest Payments
per $1,000 of Principal

Term	Contract Interest Rate (%)			
(Years)	7.00	7.25	7.50	7.75
1	86.53	86.64	86.76	86.87
2	44.77	44.89	45.00	45.11
3	30.88	30.99	31.11	31.22
4	23.95	24.06	24.18	24.30
5	19.80	19.92	20.04	20.16
6	17.05	17.17	17.29	17.41
7	15.09	15.22	15.34	15.46
8	13.63	13.76	13.88	14.01
9	12.51	12.63	12.76	12.89
10	11.61	11.74	11.87	12.00
11	10.88	11.02	11.15	11.28
12	10.28	10.42	10.55	10.69
13	9.78	9.92	10.05	10.19
14	9.35	9.49	9.63	9.77
15	8.99	9.13	9.27	9.41
16	8.67	8.81	8.96	9.10
17	8.40	8.54	8.69	8.83
18	8.16	8.30	8.45	8.60
19	7.94	8.09	8.24	8.39
20	7.75	7.90	8.06	8.21
21	7.58	7.74	7.89	8.05
22	7.43	7.59	7.75	7.90
23	7.30	7.46	7.61	7.77
24	7.18	7.34	7.50	7.66
25	7.07	7.23	7.39	7.55
26	6.97	7.13	7.29	7.46
27	6.88	7.04	7.21	7.37
28	6.80	6.96	7.13	7.30
29	6.72	6.89	7.06	7.23
30	6.65	6.82	6.99	7.16

Monthly Principal and Interest Payments
per $1,000 of Principal

Term (Years)	Contract Interest Rate (%)			
	8.00	8.25	8.50	8.75
1	86.99	87.10	87.22	87.34
2	45.23	45.34	45.46	45.57
3	31.34	31.45	31.57	31.68
4	24.41	24.53	24.65	24.77
5	20.28	20.40	20.52	20.64
6	17.53	17.66	17.78	17.90
7	15.59	15.71	15.84	15.96
8	14.14	14.26	14.39	14.52
9	13.02	13.15	13.28	13.41
10	12.13	12.27	12.40	12.53
11	11.42	11.55	11.69	11.82
12	10.82	10.96	11.10	11.24
13	10.33	10.47	10.61	10.75
14	9.91	10.06	10.20	10.34
15	9.56	9.70	9.85	9.99
16	9.25	9.40	9.54	9.69
17	8.98	9.13	9.28	9.43
18	8.75	8.90	9.05	9.21
19	8.55	8.70	8.85	9.01
20	8.36	8.52	8.68	8.84
21	8.20	8.36	8.52	8.68
22	8.06	8.22	8.38	8.55
23	7.93	8.10	8.26	8.43
24	7.82	7.98	8.15	8.32
25	7.72	7.88	8.05	8.22
26	7.63	7.79	7.96	8.13
27	7.54	7.71	7.88	8.06
28	7.47	7.64	7.81	7.99
29	7.40	7.57	7.75	7.92
30	7.34	7.51	7.69	7.87

Monthly Principal and Interest Payments
per $1,000 of Principal

Term (Years)	Contract Interest Rate (%)			
	9.00	9.25	9.50	9.75
1	87.45	87.57	87.68	87.80
2	45.68	45.80	45.91	46.03
3	31.80	31.92	32.03	32.15
4	24.88	25.00	25.12	25.24
5	20.76	20.88	21.00	21.12
6	18.03	18.15	18.27	18.40
7	16.09	16.22	16.34	16.47
8	14.65	14.78	14.91	15.04
9	13.54	13.68	13.81	13.94
10	12.67	12.80	12.94	13.08
11	11.96	12.10	12.24	12.38
12	11.38	11.52	11.66	11.81
13	10.90	11.04	11.19	11.33
14	10.49	10.64	10.78	10.93
15	10.14	10.29	10.44	10.59
16	9.85	10.00	10.15	10.30
17	9.59	9.74	9.90	10.05
18	9.36	9.52	9.68	9.84
19	9.17	9.33	9.49	9.65
20	9.00	9.16	9.32	9.49
21	8.85	9.01	9.17	9.34
22	8.71	8.88	9.04	9.21
23	8.59	8.76	8.93	9.10
24	8.49	8.66	8.83	9.00
25	8.39	8.56	8.74	8.91
26	8.31	8.48	8.66	8.83
27	8.23	8.41	8.58	8.76
28	8.16	8.34	8.52	8.70
29	8.10	8.28	8.46	8.64
30	8.05	8.23	8.41	8.59

Monthly Principal and Interest Payments
per $1,000 of Principal

Term (Years)	Contract Interest Rate (%)			
	10.00	10.25	10.50	10.75
1	87.92	88.03	88.15	88.27
2	46.15	46.26	46.38	46.49
3	32.27	32.38	32.50	32.62
4	25.36	25.48	25.60	25.72
5	21.25	21.37	21.49	21.62
6	18.53	18.65	18.78	18.91
7	16.60	16.73	16.86	16.99
8	15.17	15.31	15.44	15.57
9	14.08	14.21	14.35	14.49
10	13.22	13.35	13.49	13.63
11	12.52	12.66	12.80	12.95
12	11.95	12.10	12.24	12.39
13	11.48	11.63	11.78	11.92
14	11.08	11.23	11.38	11.54
15	10.75	10.90	11.05	11.21
16	10.46	10.62	10.77	10.93
17	10.21	10.37	10.53	10.69
18	10.00	10.16	10.32	10.49
19	9.81	9.98	10.14	10.31
20	9.65	9.82	9.98	10.15
21	9.51	9.68	9.85	10.02
22	9.38	9.55	9.73	9.90
23	9.27	9.44	9.62	9.79
24	9.17	9.35	9.52	9.70
25	9.09	9.26	9.44	9.62
26	9.01	9.19	9.37	9.55
27	8.94	9.12	9.30	9.49
28	8.88	9.06	9.25	9.43
29	8.82	9.01	9.19	9.38
30	8.78	8.96	9.15	9.33

Monthly Principal and Interest Payments
per $1,000 of Principal

Term (Years)	Contract Interest Rate (%)			
	11.00	11.25	11.50	11.75
1	88.38	88.50	88.62	88.73
2	46.61	46.72	46.84	46.96
3	32.74	32.86	32.98	33.10
4	25.85	25.97	26.09	26.21
5	21.74	21.87	21.99	22.12
6	19.03	19.16	19.29	19.42
7	17.12	17.25	17.39	17.52
8	15.71	15.84	15.98	16.12
9	14.63	14.76	14.90	15.04
10	13.77	13.92	14.06	14.20
11	13.09	13.24	13.38	13.53
12	12.54	12.68	12.83	12.98
13	12.08	12.23	12.38	12.53
14	11.69	11.85	12.00	12.16
15	11.37	11.52	11.68	11.84
16	11.09	11.25	11.41	11.57
17	10.85	11.02	11.18	11.35
18	10.65	10.82	10.98	11.15
19	10.47	10.64	10.81	10.98
20	10.32	10.49	10.66	10.84
21	10.19	10.36	10.54	10.71
22	10.07	10.25	10.42	10.60
23	9.97	10.15	10.33	10.51
24	9.88	10.06	10.24	10.42
25	9.80	9.98	10.16	10.35
26	9.73	9.91	10.10	10.28
27	9.67	9.85	10.04	10.23
28	9.61	9.80	9.99	10.18
29	9.57	9.75	9.94	10.13
30	9.52	9.71	9.90	10.09

Monthly Principal and Interest Payments
per $1,000 of Principal

Term (Years)	Contract Interest Rate (%)			
	12.00	12.25	12.50	12.75
1	88.85	88.97	89.08	89.20
2	47.07	47.19	47.31	47.42
3	33.21	33.33	33.45	33.57
4	26.33	26.46	26.58	26.70
5	22.24	22.37	22.50	22.63
6	19.55	19.68	19.81	19.94
7	17.65	17.79	17.92	18.06
8	16.25	16.39	16.53	16.67
9	15.18	15.33	15.47	15.61
10	14.35	14.49	14.64	14.78
11	13.68	13.83	13.98	14.13
12	13.13	13.29	13.44	13.59
13	12.69	12.84	13.00	13.15
14	12.31	12.47	12.63	12.79
15	12.00	12.16	12.33	12.49
16	11.74	11.90	12.07	12.23
17	11.51	11.68	11.85	12.02
18	11.32	11.49	11.66	11.83
19	11.15	11.33	11.50	11.67
20	11.01	11.19	11.36	11.54
21	10.89	11.06	11.24	11.42
22	10.78	10.96	11.14	11.32
23	10.69	10.87	11.05	11.23
24	10.60	10.79	10.97	11.16
25	10.53	10.72	10.90	11.09
26	10.47	10.66	10.84	11.03
27	10.41	10.60	10.79	10.98
28	10.37	10.56	10.75	10.94
29	10.32	10.52	10.71	10.90
30	10.29	10.48	10.67	10.87

Monthly Principal and Interest Payments
per $1,000 of Principal

Term	Contract Interest Rate (%)			
(Years)	13.00	13.25	13.50	13.75
1	89.32	89.43	89.55	89.67
2	47.54	47.66	47.78	47.90
3	33.69	33.81	33.94	34.06
4	26.83	26.95	27.08	27.20
5	22.75	22.88	23.01	23.14
6	20.07	20.21	20.34	20.47
7	18.19	18.33	18.46	18.60
8	16.81	16.95	17.09	17.23
9	15.75	15.90	16.04	16.19
10	14.93	15.08	15.23	15.38
11	14.28	14.43	14.58	14.73
12	13.75	13.90	14.06	14.21
13	13.31	13.47	13.63	13.79
14	12.95	13.11	13.28	13.44
15	12.65	12.82	12.98	13.15
16	12.40	12.57	12.74	12.91
17	12.19	12.36	12.53	12.70
18	12.00	12.18	12.35	12.53
19	11.85	12.03	12.20	12.38
20	11.72	11.89	12.07	12.25
21	11.60	11.78	11.96	12.15
22	11.50	11.69	11.87	12.05
23	11.42	11.60	11.79	11.97
24	11.34	11.53	11.72	11.91
25	11.28	11.47	11.66	11.85
26	11.22	11.41	11.60	11.80
27	11.17	11.37	11.56	11.75
28	11.13	11.32	11.52	11.71
29	11.09	11.29	11.48	11.68
30	11.06	11.26	11.45	11.65

Monthly Principal and Interest Payments
per $1,000 of Principal

Term (Years)	Contract Interest Rate (%)			
	14.00	14.25	14.50	14.75
1	89.79	89.90	90.02	90.14
2	48.01	48.13	48.25	48.37
3	34.18	34.30	34.42	34.54
4	27.33	27.45	27.58	27.70
5	23.27	23.40	23.53	23.66
6	20.61	20.74	20.87	21.01
7	18.74	18.88	19.02	19.16
8	17.37	17.51	17.66	17.80
9	16.33	16.48	16.63	16.78
10	15.53	15.68	15.83	15.98
11	14.89	15.04	15.20	15.35
12	14.37	14.53	14.69	14.85
13	13.95	14.11	14.28	14.44
14	13.60	13.77	13.94	14.10
15	13.32	13.49	13.66	13.83
16	13.08	13.25	13.42	13.59
17	12.87	13.05	13.22	13.40
18	12.70	12.88	13.06	13.24
19	12.56	12.74	12.92	13.10
20	12.44	12.62	12.80	12.98
21	12.33	12.51	12.70	12.88
22	12.24	12.43	12.61	12.80
23	12.16	12.35	12.54	12.73
24	12.10	12.29	12.48	12.67
25	12.04	12.23	12.42	12.61
26	11.99	12.18	12.38	12.57
27	11.95	12.14	12.34	12.53
28	11.91	12.10	12.30	12.50
29	11.88	12.07	12.27	12.47
30	11.85	12.05	12.25	12.44

INDEX

BARRON'S BUSINESS KEYS Each "key" explains approximately 50 concepts and provides a glossary and index. Each book: Paperback, approx. 160 pp., 4¾₆" x 7", $4.95, $5.95, & $7.95 Can. $6.50, $7.95, $8.50, & $11.50.

Available at bookstores, or by mail from Barron's. Enclose check or money order for full amount plus sales tax where applicable and 18% for postage & handling (minimum charge $5.95). Prices subject to change without notice. $= U.S. dollars • Can. $= Canadian dollars • Barron's ISBN Prefix 0-8120, *indicates 0-7641

Barron's Educational Series, Inc.
250 Wireless Boulevard • Hauppauge, NY 11788
In Canada: Georgetown Book Warehouse
34 Armstrong Avenue, Georgetown, Ont. L7G 4R9
www.barronseduc.com

(#10) R 6/00